MY First
Motivational
Print Handwriting Workbook

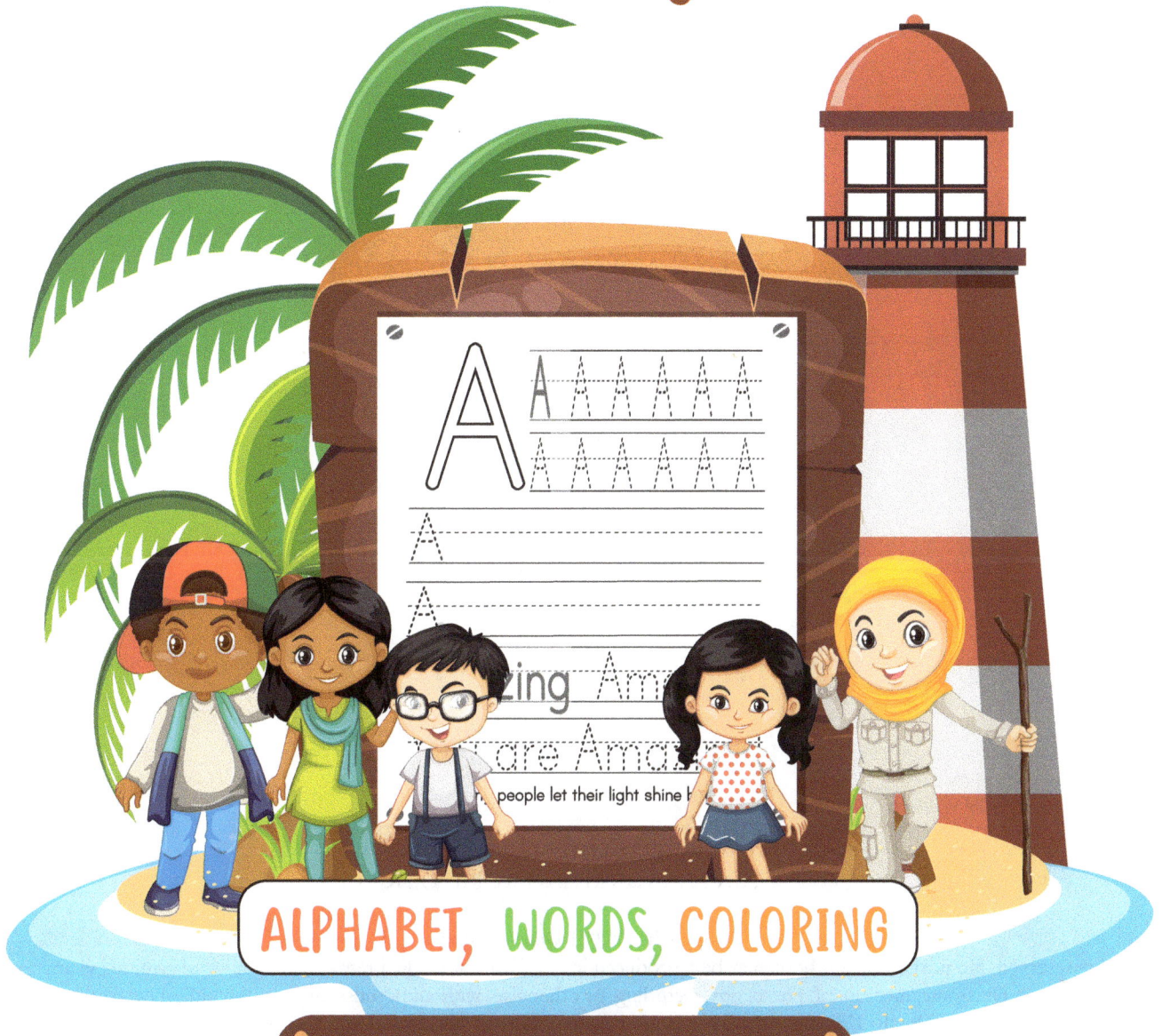

A
A A A A A A A
A A A A A A A

A

A

...zing Am...

...re Ama...

...people let their light shine b...

ALPHABET, WORDS, COLORING

Dr. Denisha Brown
FAN Educational Services, LLC

MY FIRST MOTIVATIONAL
PRINT HANDWRITING WORKBOOK

ISBN: 979-8-9858105-0-9

This Book Belongs To

_____

_____

Author's Message

The power of learning and motivational words are very valuable to the young minds of children of all ages.

I am Dr. Denisha Brown, an educational leader and educational consultant. I have taught grades K-5 in a public school setting in the southeastern part of the United States of America. Upon completing my years of teaching, I furthered my career as a School Counselor eager to help children's academic and social-emotional development. Therefore, as I reflected on how I could support children in this technological era, I became aware of students lack of penmanship. I also, observed and researched the development of children's self-esteem and confidence.

Based upon my research and observations, I present to you and your child my workbook. I hope this workbook provides handwriting support for your child, teaches them new vocabulary, and builds their self-esteem and confidence to be the best student they can be!

Let's spread positivity in the world!

Dr. Brown

HELPFUL SUGGESTIONS

My First Motivational Print Handwriting Workbook was created to reinforce extra practice with handwriting.

The purpose of the motivational words aligned with each alphabet is to increase the self-esteem of children. It is vital that children hear and receive 5 or more positive praises for every 1 corrective interaction for negative behavior. This workbook is going to help improve handwriting skills, build vocabulary, and build your child's self-esteem and confidence. I thank you for your purchase and hope you and your child enjoy.

1. Allow your child to practice handwriting skills at least 3 times a week.
2. If your child struggles with making letters by writing try using shaving cream or sand. This will allow your child to feel the movement of letter making.
3. Use the activity page for cutting pictures out of magazines, printing pictures, or drawing pictures that begin with each letter.
4. You can extend the activity page by naming the objects placed there. Ask your child to use the name of each object in a sentence.
5. Ask your child to find the different objects that begin with the letter of practice on each coloring sheet.
6. Have your child say the Daily Affirmations to increase your child's self-esteem and confidence.

Trace each letter and word. Practice writing each letter on your own.

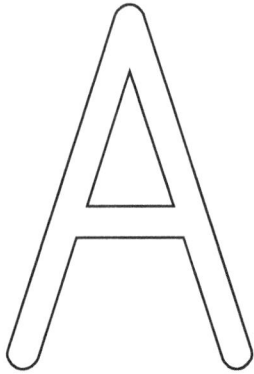

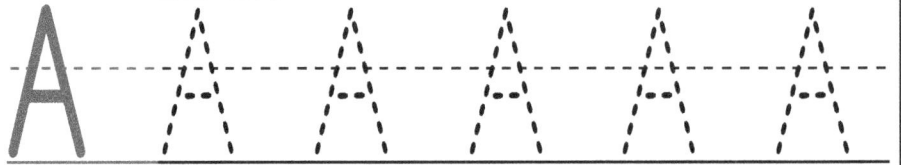

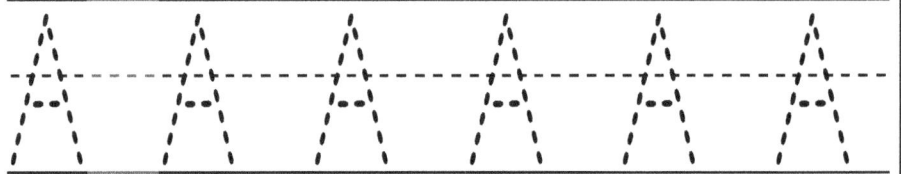

A   A   A   A   A   A   A   A

A   A   A   A   A   A   A

A

A

Amazing   Amazing

You are Amazing!

Amazing people let their light shine bright.

Trace each letter and word. Practice writing each letter on your own.

a a a a a a

a a a a a a

a

a

a

amazing amazing

Be amazing!

Amazing people let their light shine bright.

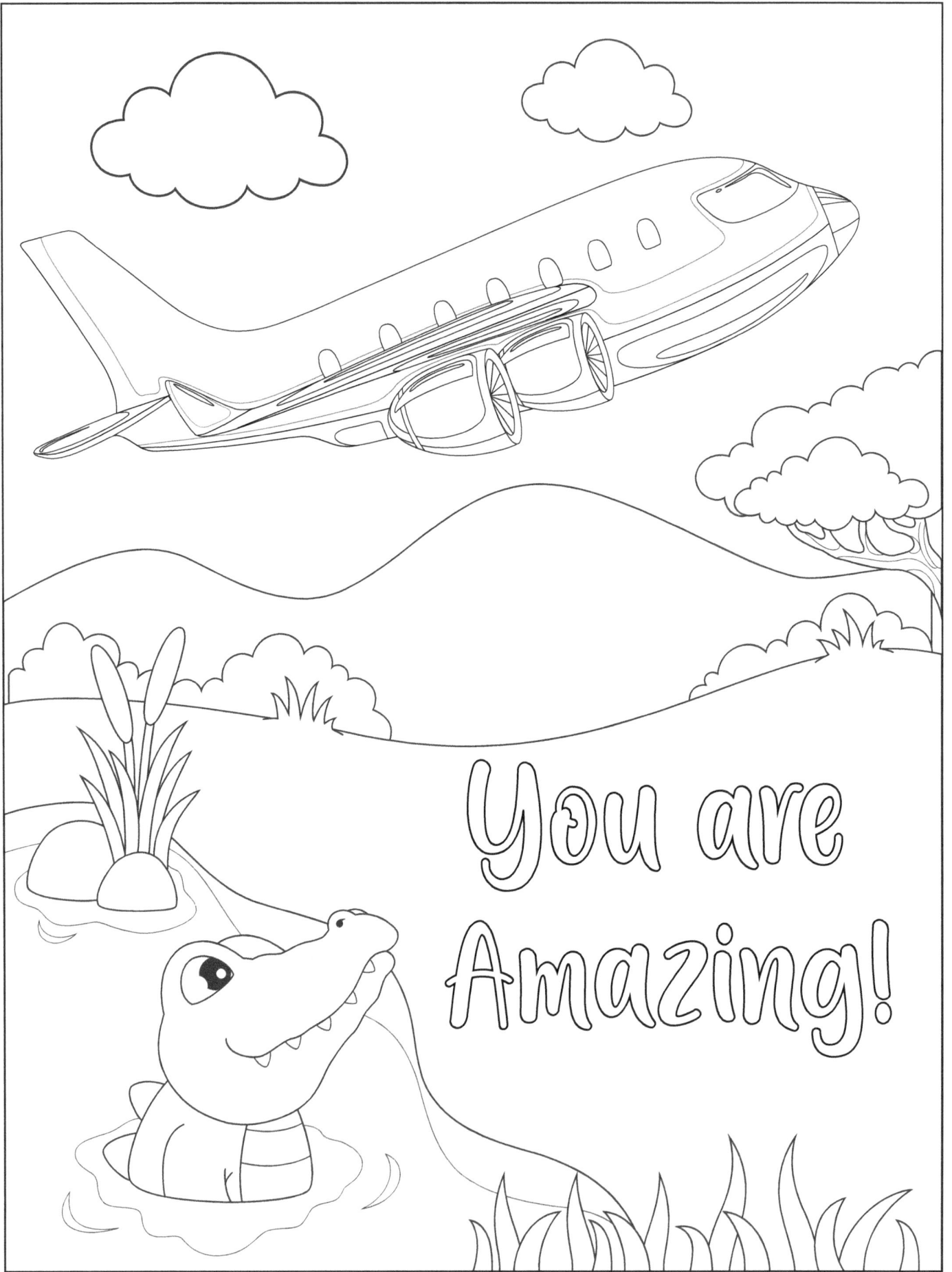

You are
Amazing!

Name:_____ Date:_____

Draw items that start with the letter in the box. You may also find pictures that start with the letter and paste the pictures here.

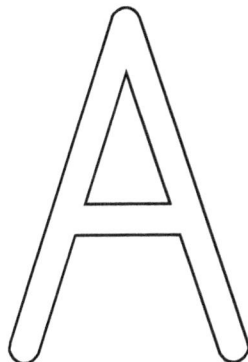

A

Trace each letter and word. Practice writing each letter on your own.

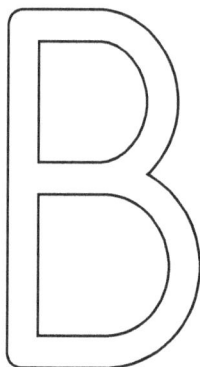

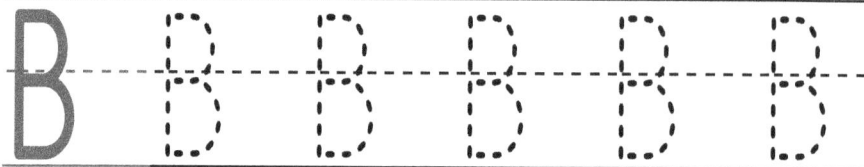

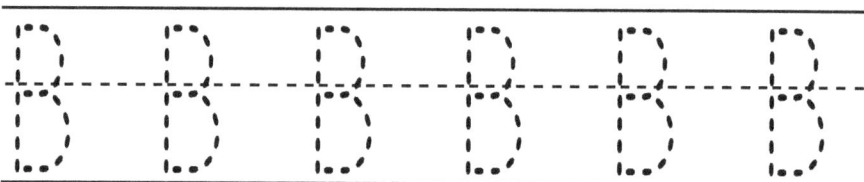

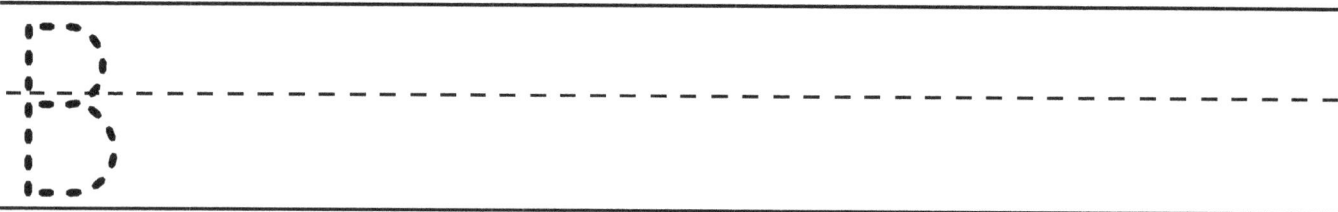

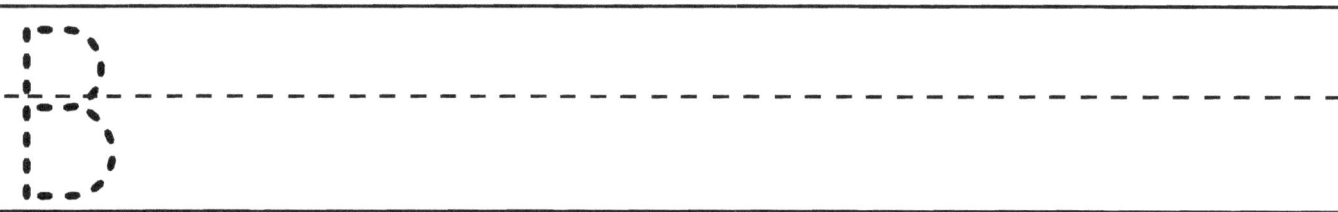

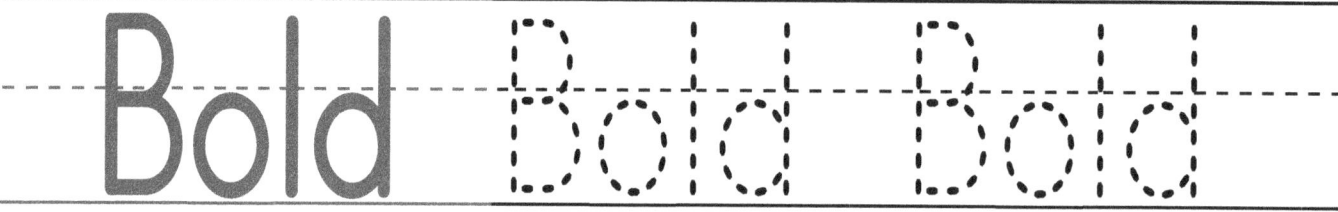

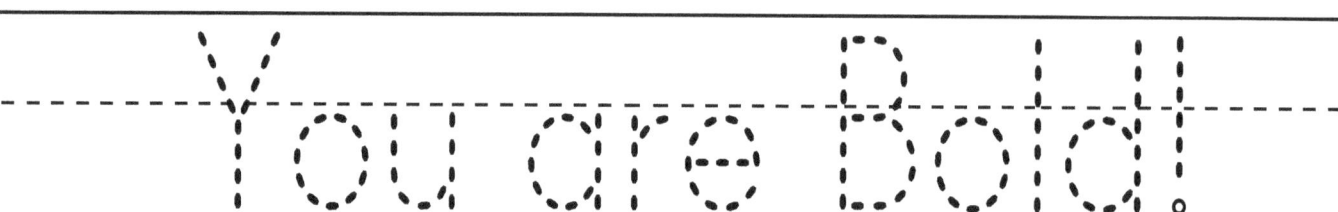

B

B B B B B B

B B B B B B

B

B

Bold Bold Bold

You are Bold!

Make positive bold and beautiful choices for your life.

Name:_____   Date:_____

Trace each letter and word. Practice writing each letter on your own.

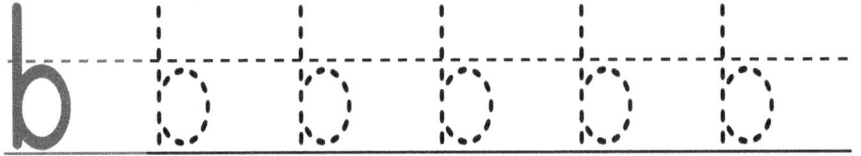

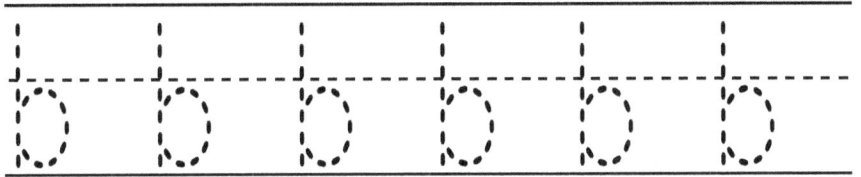

b   b b b b b

b b b b b b

b

b

bold   bold bold

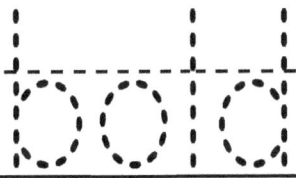

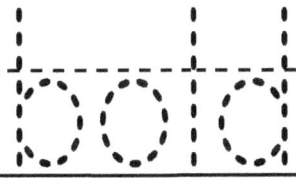

Be bold and beautiful!

Make positive bold and beautiful choices for your life.

Be
Bold!

Name:_____ Date:_____

Draw items that start with the letter in the box. You may also find pictures that start with the letter and paste the pictures here.

B

Trace each letter and word. Practice writing each letter on your own.

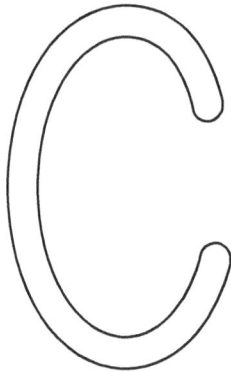

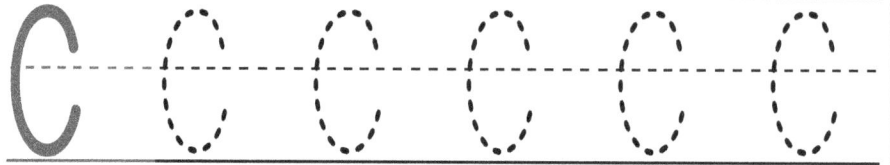

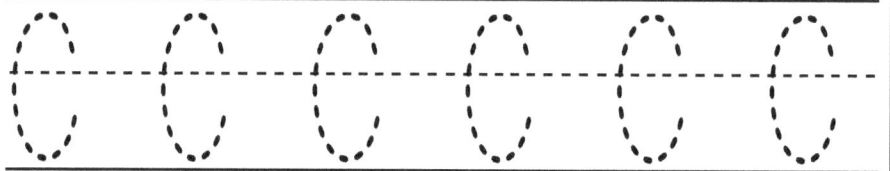

C   C c c c c c c

     c c c c c c

c

c

Courageous Courageous

You are Courageous!

Show that you are courageous by showing who you really are daily.

Trace each letter and word. Practice writing each letter on your own.

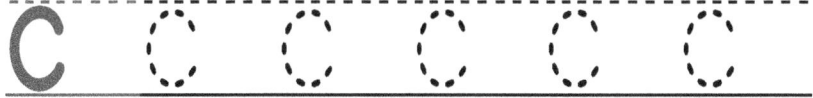

C

c c c c c c

c c c c c c

c

c

courageous courageous

Be courageous!

Show that you are courageous by showing who you really are daily.

You are

Courageous!

Name:_____ Date:_____

Draw items that start with the letter in the box. You may also find pictures that start with the letter and paste the pictures here.

C

Trace each letter and word. Practice writing each letter on your own.

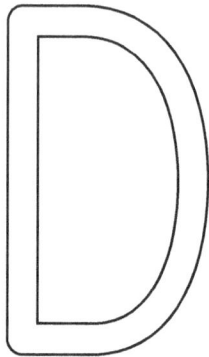

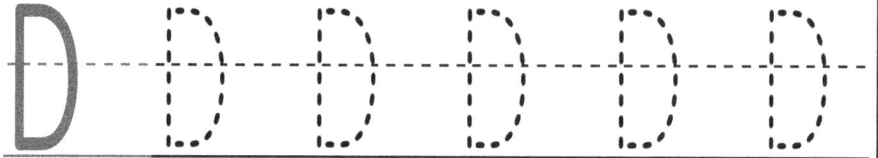

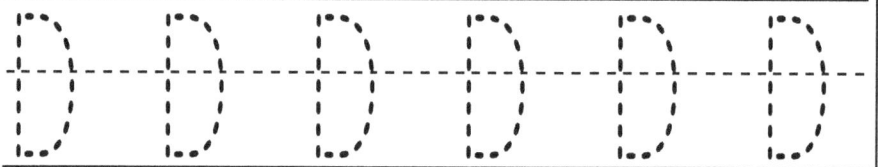

D   D D D D D D

D D D D D D

D

D

Determined Determined

You are Determined!

Always be determined to learn and to reach for your dreams.

Trace each letter and word. Practice writing each letter on your own.

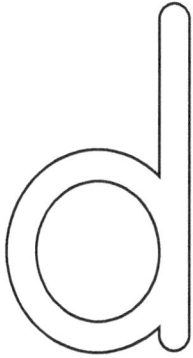

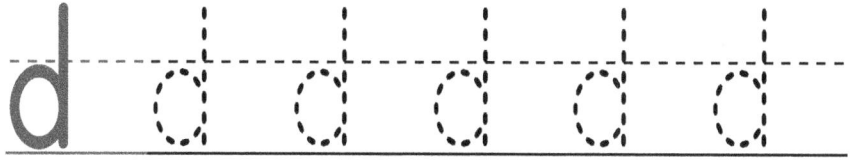

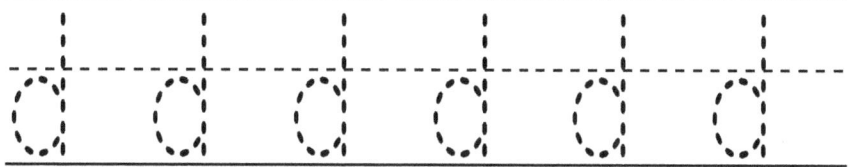

d   d d d d d

d d d d d d

d

d

determined   determined

Be determined!

Always be determined to learn and to reach for your dreams.

Be Determined!

Name:_____ Date:_____

Draw items that start with the letter in the box. You may also find pictures that start with the letter and paste the pictures here.

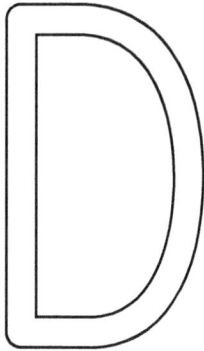

D

Trace each letter and word. Practice writing each letter on your own.

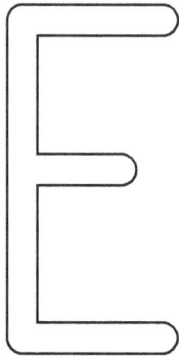

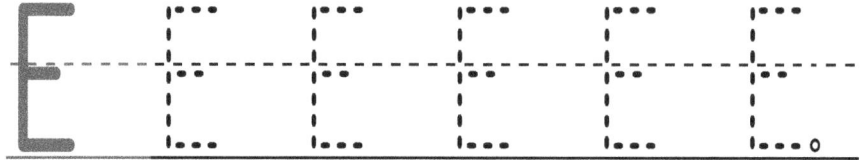

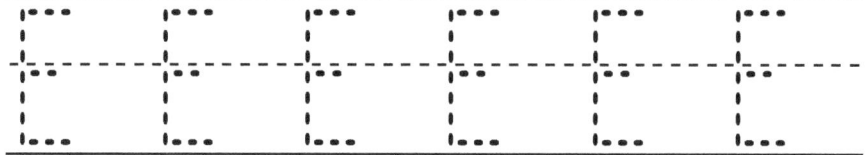

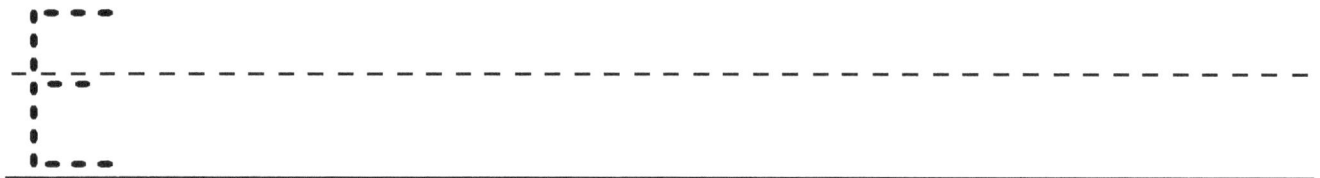

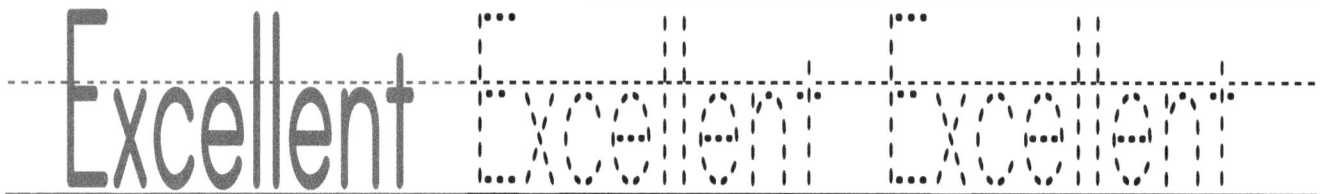

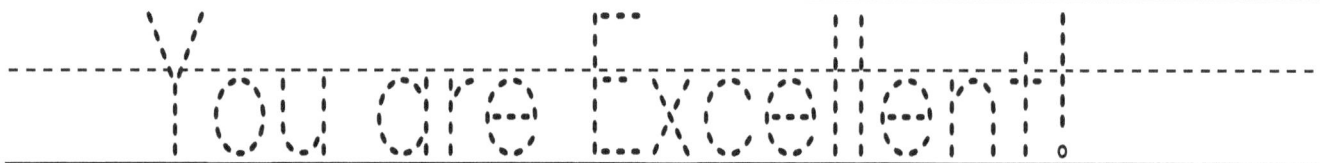

E

E E E E E E

E E E E E E

E

E

Excellent Excellent Excellent

You are Excellent!

Show how excellent you are in everything you do.

Trace each letter and word. Practice writing each letter on your own.

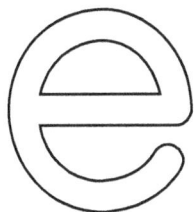

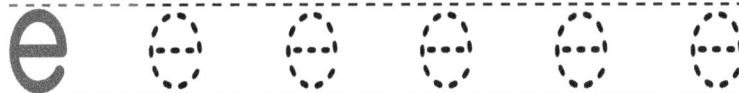

e   e   e   e   e   e

e

e   e   e   e   e   e

e

e

excellent excellent excellent

Be excellent!

Show how excellent you are in everything you do.

You are Excellent!

Name:_____ Date:_____

Draw items that start with the letter in the box. You may also find pictures that start with the letter and paste the pictures here.

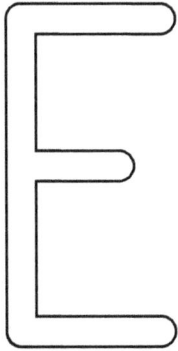

E

Trace each letter and word. Practice writing each letter on your own.

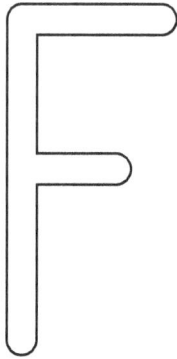

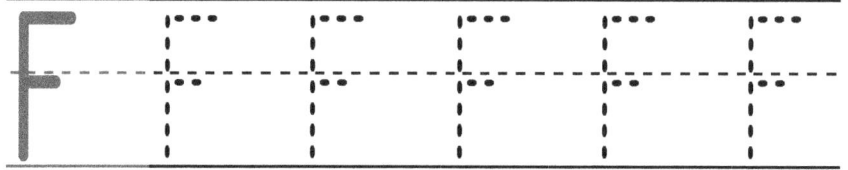

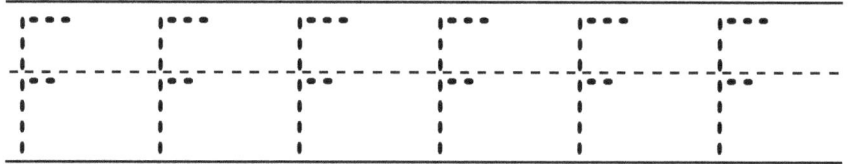

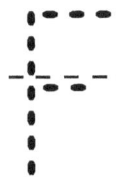

F

F F F F F F

F F F F F F

F

F

Fantastic Fantastic Fantastic

You are Fantastic!

Believe that fantastic things will happen in your life.

Name:_____ Date:_____

Trace each letter and word. Practice writing each letter on your own.

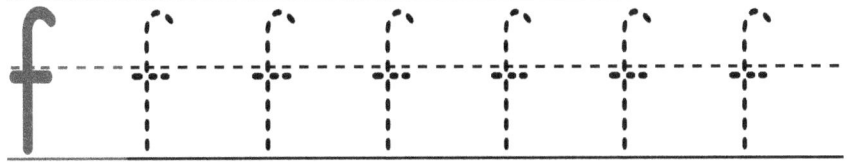

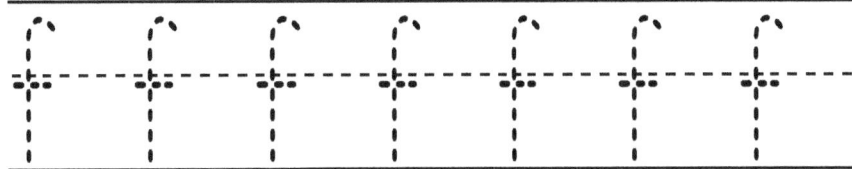

f   f f f f f f

f f f f f f

f

f

fantastic fantastic fantastic

Be fantastic!

Believe that fantastic things will happen in your life.

Be Fantastic!

Name:_____ Date:_____

Draw items that start with the letter in the box. You may also find pictures that start with the letter and paste the pictures here.

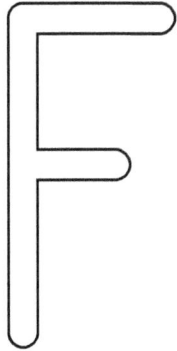

F

Trace each letter and word. Practice writing each letter on your own.

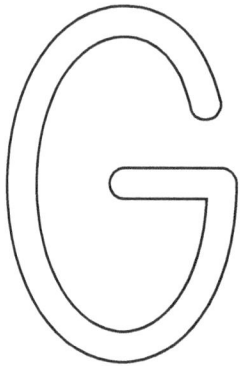

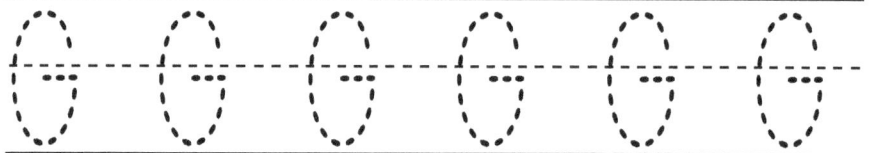

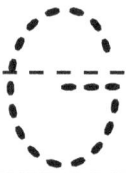

G   G G G G G G

G G G G G G

G

G

Gifted   Gifted Gifted Gifted

You are Gifted!

Everyone has a gift, when you find yours use it to the fullest.

Name:_____ Date:_____

Trace each letter and word. Practice writing each letter on your own.

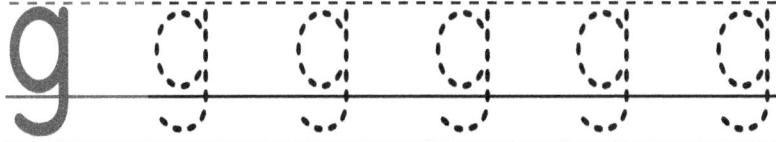

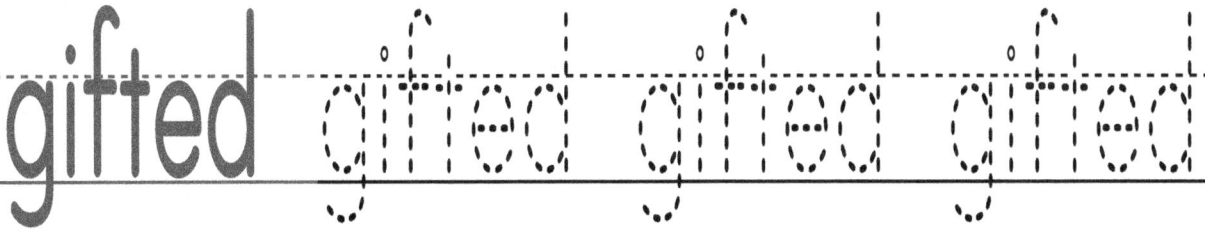

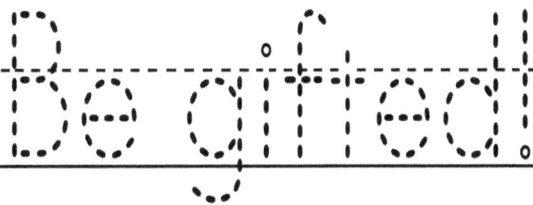

g   g g g g g g
     g g g g g g

g

g

gifted   gifted gifted gifted
          Be gifted!

Everyone has a gift, when you find yours use it to the fullest.

You are gifted!

Name:_____ Date:_____

Draw items that start with the letter in the box. You may also find pictures that start with the letter and paste the pictures here.

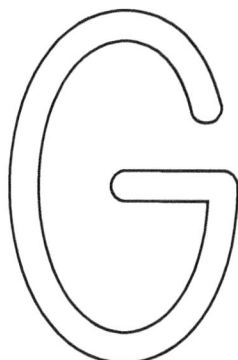

G

Trace each letter and word. Practice writing each letter on your own.

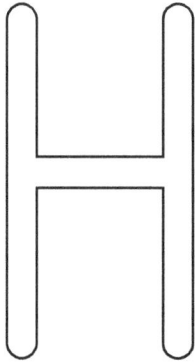

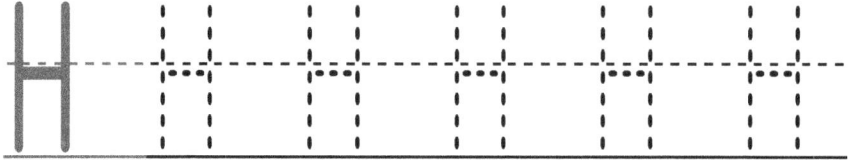

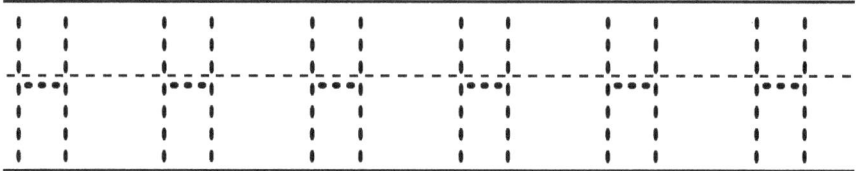

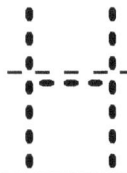

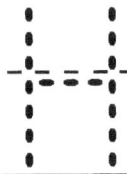

H

H   H   H   H   H   H

H   H   H   H   H   H

H

H

Honest Honest Honest

You are Honest!

When you are honest people will trust you more.

Trace each letter and word. Practice writing each letter on your own.

h

h h h h h h

h h h h h h

h

h

honest honest honest

Be honest!

When you are honest people will trust you more.

Name:_____ Date:_____

Draw items that start with the letter in the box. You may also find pictures that start with the letter and paste the pictures here.

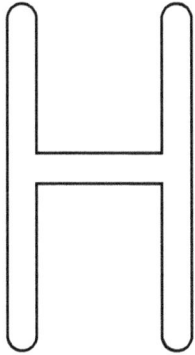

H

Trace each letter and word. Practice writing each letter on your own.

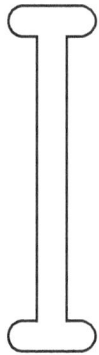

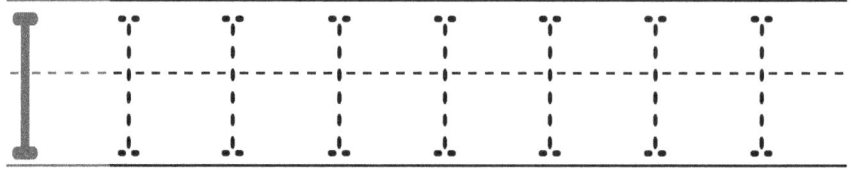

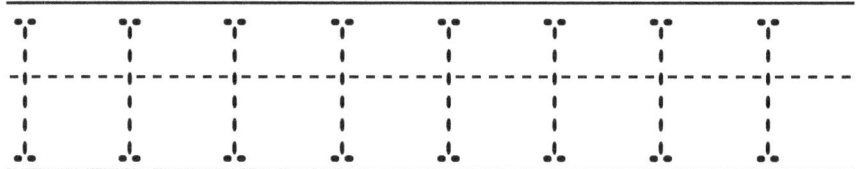

I   I I I I I I I

I I I I I I I

I

I

Intelligent Intelligent

You are Intelligent!

Surround yourself with intelligent friends just like you.

Trace each letter and word. Practice writing each letter on your own.

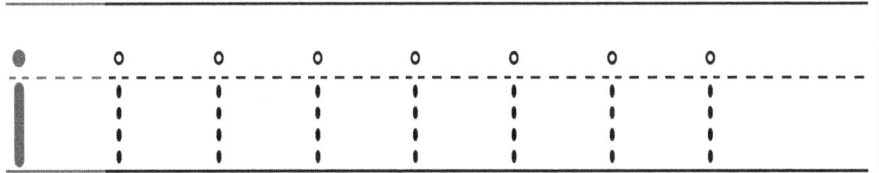

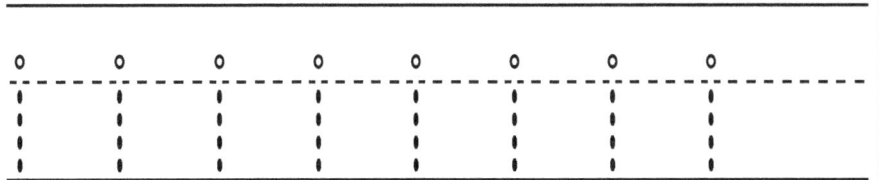

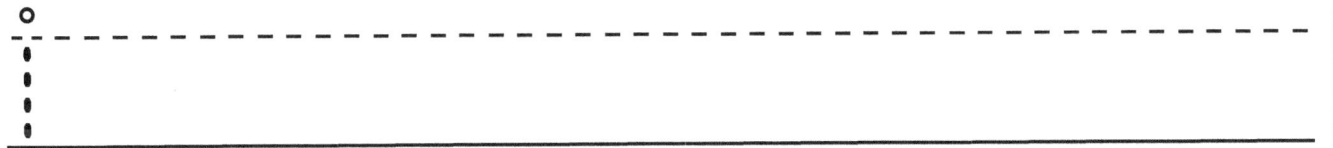

i

i i i i i i i i

i i i i i i i i

intelligent intelligent

Be intelligent!

Surround yourself with intelligent friends just like you.

You are Intelligent!

Name:_____ Date:_____

Draw items that start with the letter in the box. You may also find pictures that start with the letter and paste the pictures here.

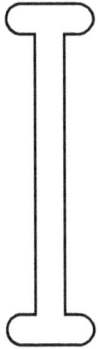

I

Trace each letter and word. Practice writing each letter on your own.

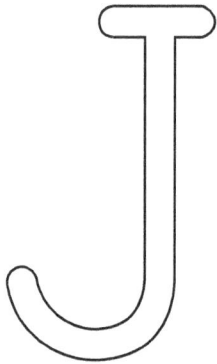

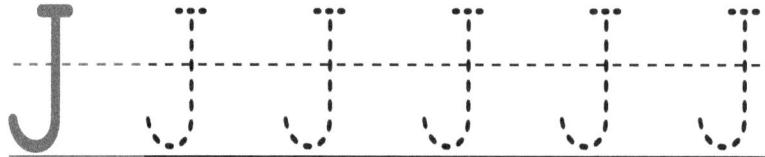

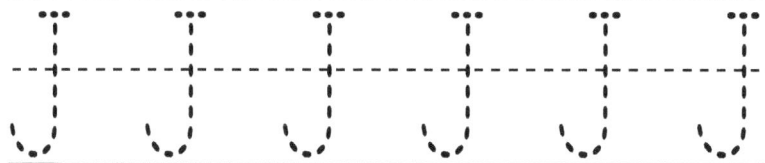

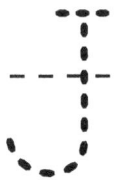

J

J J J J J J J

J J J J J J J

J

J

Jewel Jewel Jewel

You are Jewel!

You are a jewel to the world.

Trace each letter and word. Practice writing each letter on your own.

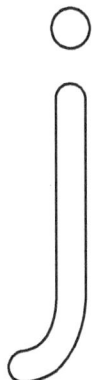

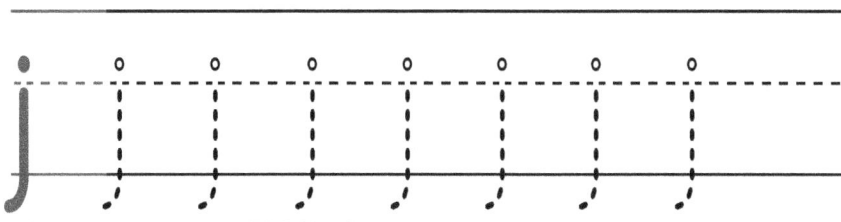

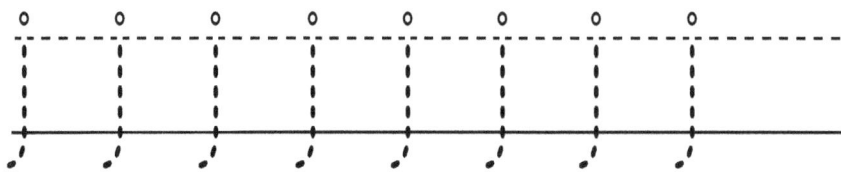

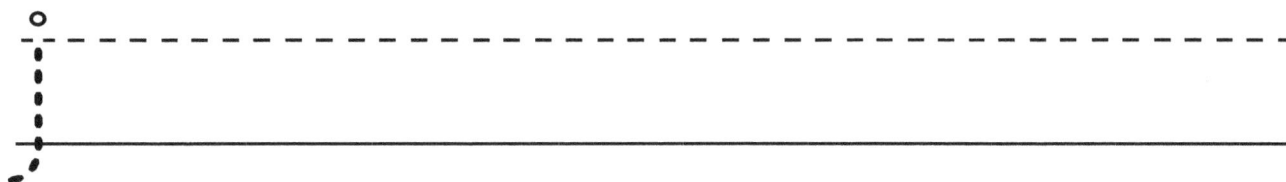

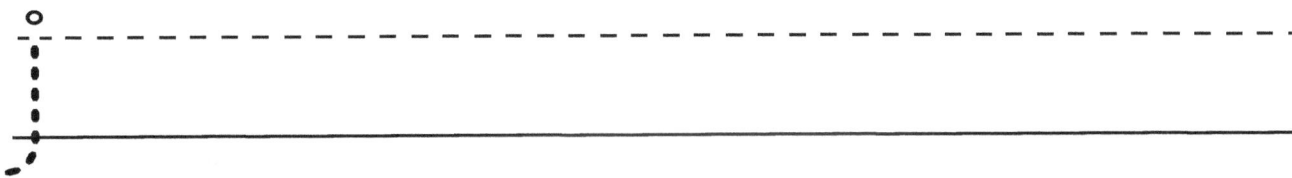

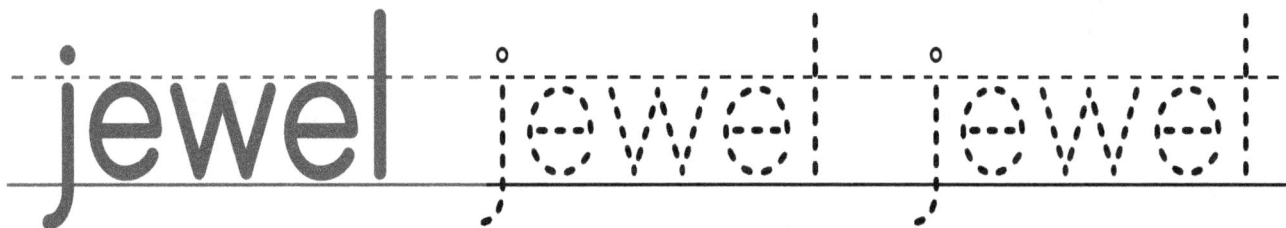

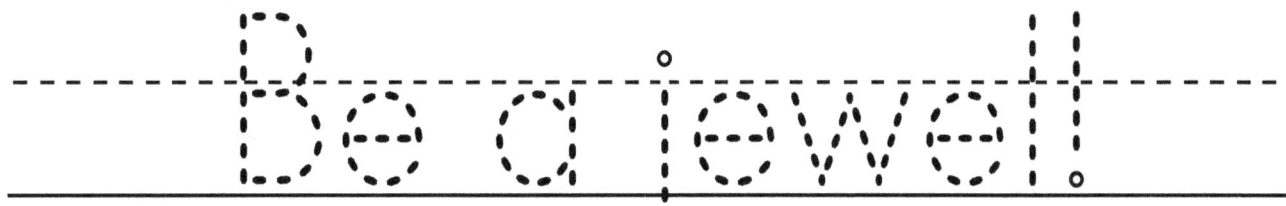

j   j j j j j j j j

j j j j j j j j

jewel   jewel jewel

Be a jewel!

You are a jewel to the world.

Name:_____ Date:_____

Draw items that start with the letter in the box. You may also find pictures that start with the letter and paste the pictures here.

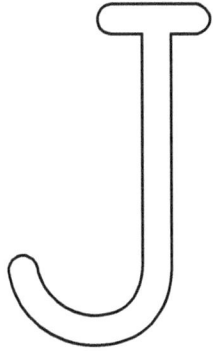

J

Trace each letter and word. Practice writing each letter on your own.

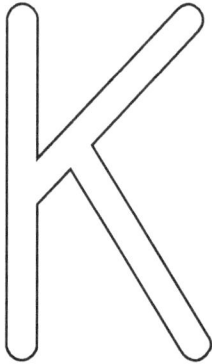

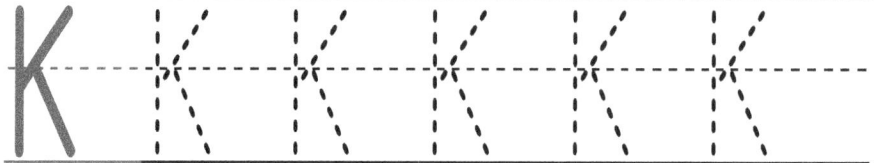

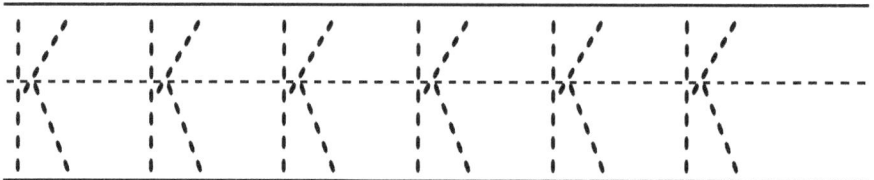

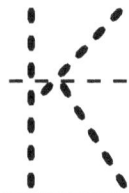

K

K K K K K K

K K K K K K

K

K

Kind Kind Kind

You are Kind!

You are one of a kind and it shows in your acts of kindness.

Trace each letter and word. Practice writing each letter on your own.

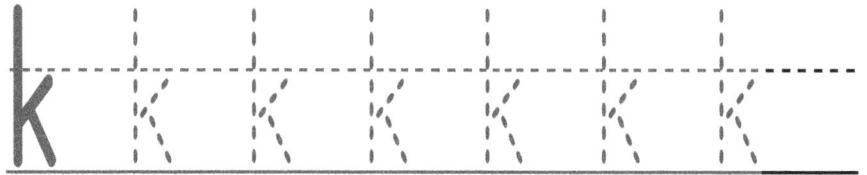

k   k k k k k k k

k k k k k k k

k

k

kind   kind kind

Be kind!

You are one of a kind and it shows in your acts of kindness.

YOU ARE KIND!

Draw items that start with the letter in the box. You may also find pictures that start with the letter and paste the pictures here.

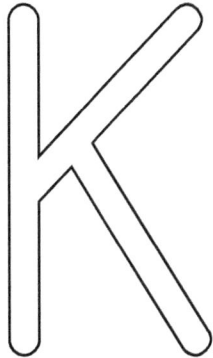

K

Trace each letter and word. Practice writing each letter on your own.

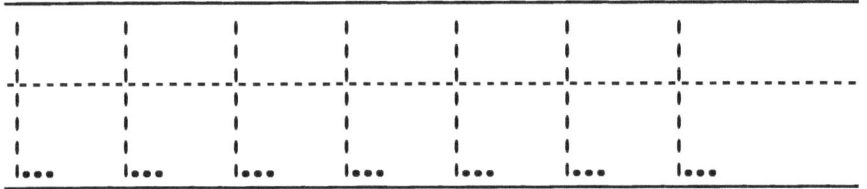

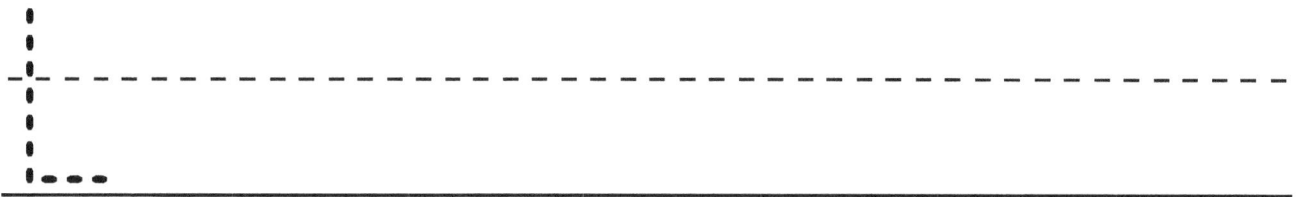

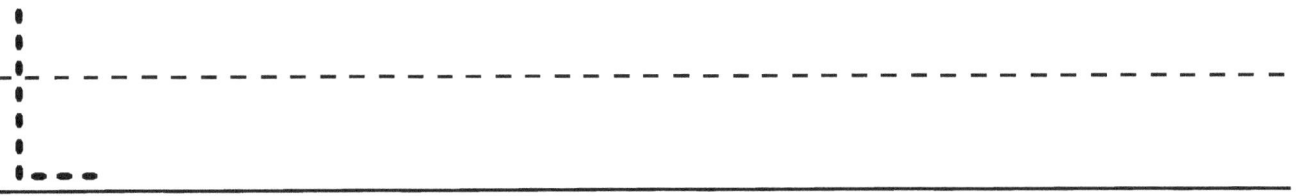

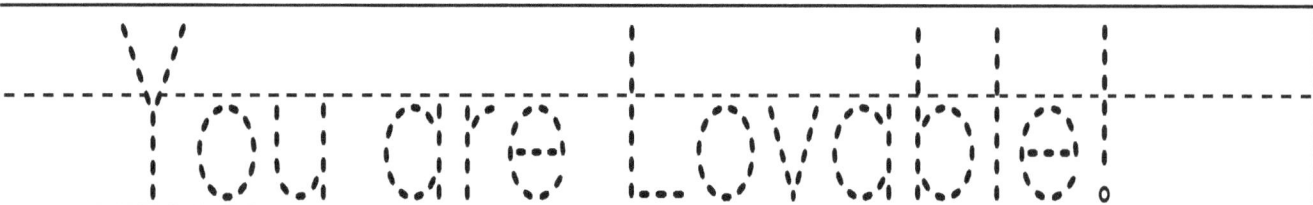

L

L L L L L L L

L L L L L L L

L

L

Lovable Lovable

You are Lovable!

You show many admirable and lovable traits.

Trace each letter and word. Practice writing each letter on your own.

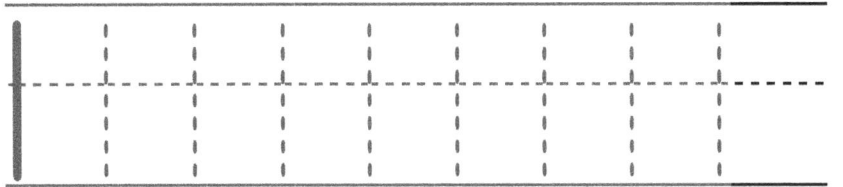

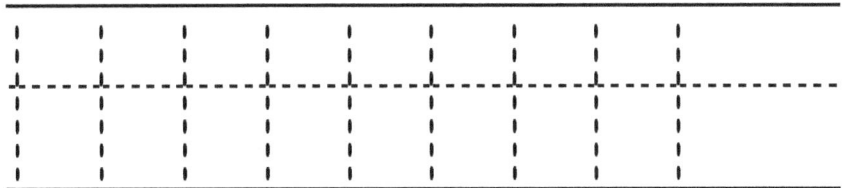

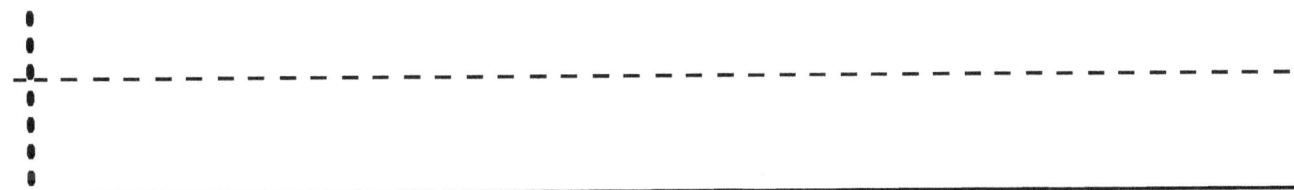

lovable lovable

Be lovable!

You show many admirable and lovable traits.

Be lovable!

Name:_____ Date:_____

Draw items that start with the letter in the box. You may also find pictures that start with the letter and paste the pictures here.

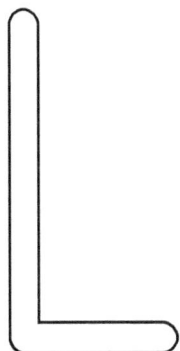

L

Trace each letter and word. Practice writing each letter on your own.

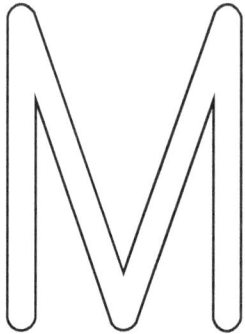

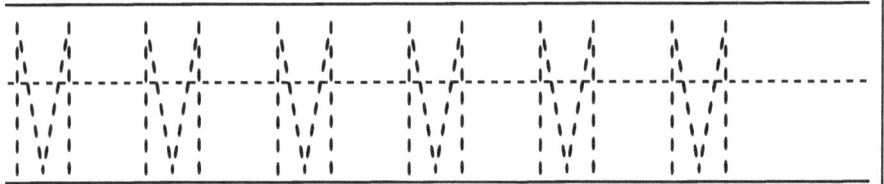

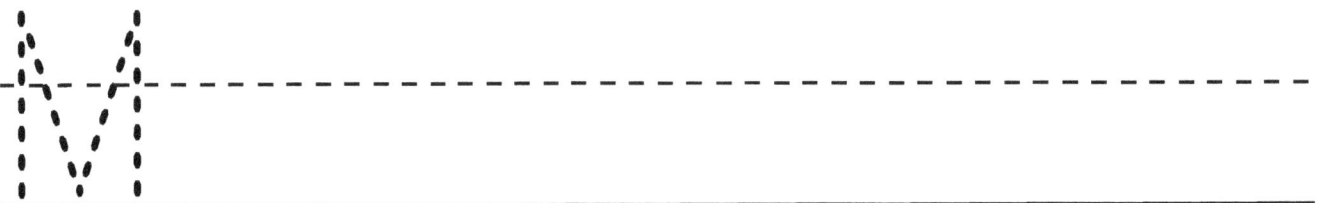

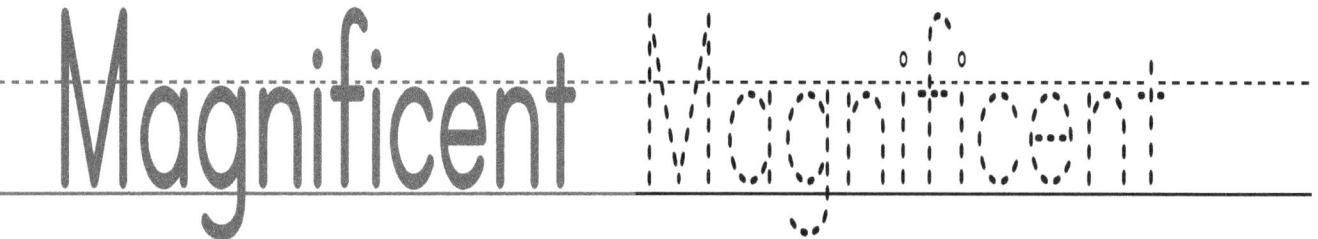

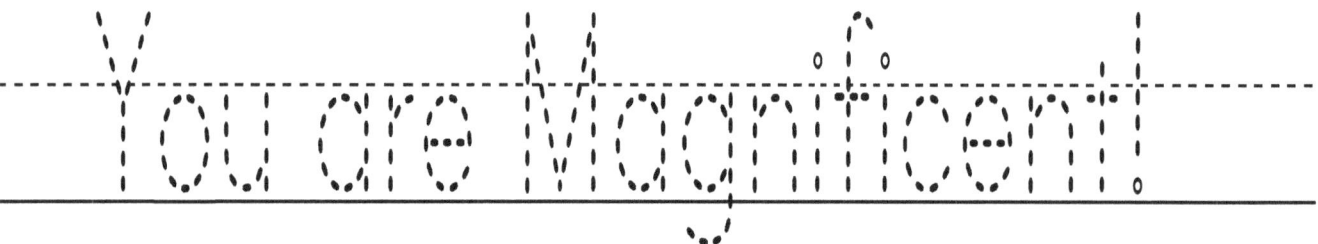

M

M M M M M M

M M M M M M

M

M

Magnificent Magnificent

You are Magnificent!

The ideas and dreams you have are magnificent.

Trace each letter and word. Practice writing each letter on your own.

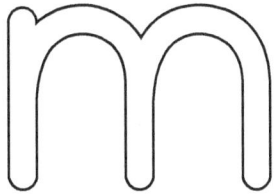

m   m m m m m m

m m m m m m

m

m

magnificent magnificent

Be magnificent!

The ideas and dreams you have are magnificent.

YOU ARE MAGNIFICENT!

Name:_____ Date:_____

Draw items that start with the letter in the box. You may also find pictures that start with the letter and paste the pictures here.

M

Trace each letter and word. Practice writing each letter on your own.

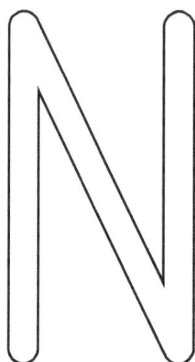

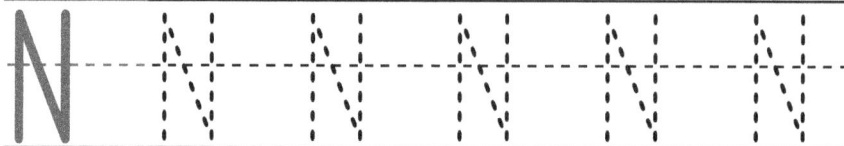

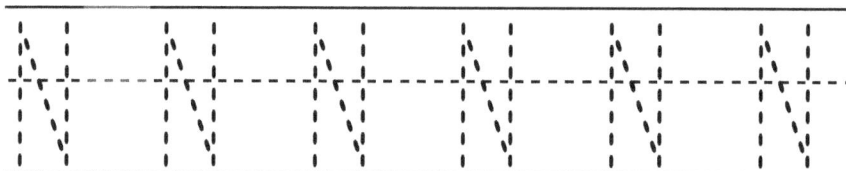

N

N   N   N   N   N   N   N

N   N   N   N   N   N   N

N

N

Noble   Noble   Noble

You are Noble!

People are inspired by your noble acts of kindness.

Trace each letter and word. Practice writing each letter on your own.

n   n n n n n n n

n n n n n n

n

n

noble   noble   noble

Be noble!

People are inspired by your noble acts of kindness.

BE NOBLE!

Name:_____ Date:_____

Draw items that start with the letter in the box. You may also find pictures that start with the letter and paste the pictures here.

N

Name:_____ Date:_____

Trace each letter and word. Practice writing each letter on your own.

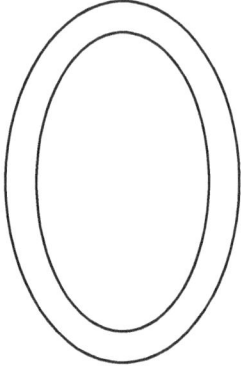

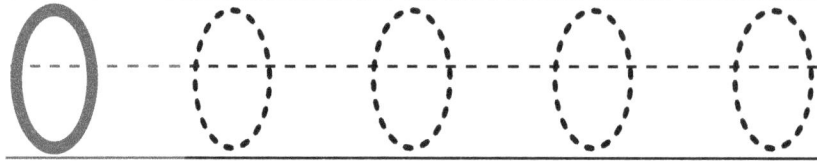

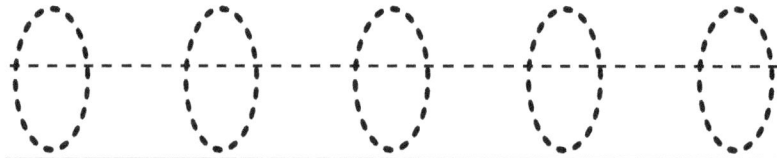

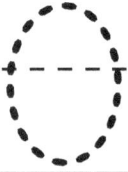

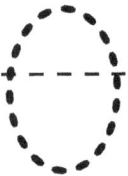

O   O   O   O   O   O

O   O   O   O   O

O

O

Original Original

You are Original!

Your style is original.

Trace each letter and word. Practice writing each letter on your own.

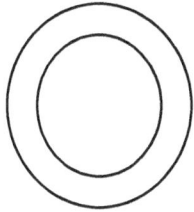

O o o o o o o

o o o o o o

o

o

original original

Be original!

Your style is original.

YOU ARE ORIGINAL!

Name:_____ Date:_____

Draw items that start with the letter in the box. You may also find pictures that start with the letter and paste the pictures here.

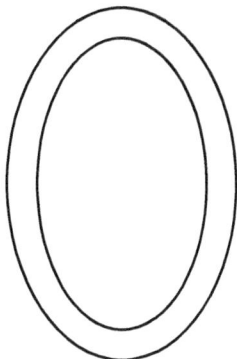

O

Trace each letter and word. Practice writing each letter on your own.

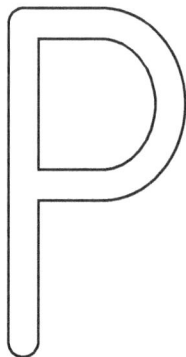

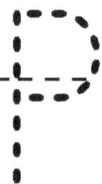

P P P P P P

P P P P P P

P

P

Powerful Powerful Powerful

You are Powerful!

The more you learn, the more powerful you will become.

Trace each letter and word. Practice writing each letter on your own.

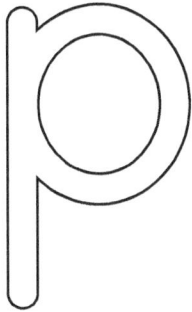

p   p p p p p p

p p p p p p

p

p

powerful powerful

Be powerful!

The more you learn, the more powerful you will become.

BE POWERFUL!

Name:_____ Date:_____

Draw items that start with the letter in the box. You may also find pictures that start with the letter and paste the pictures here.

P

Trace each letter and word. Practice writing each letter on your own.

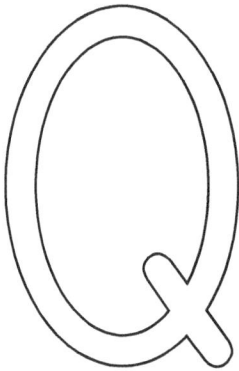

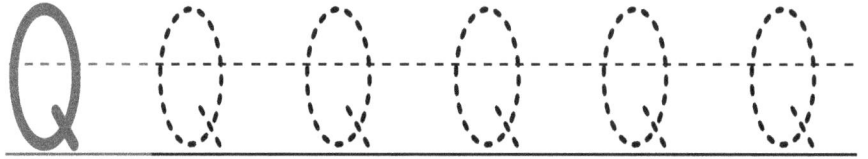

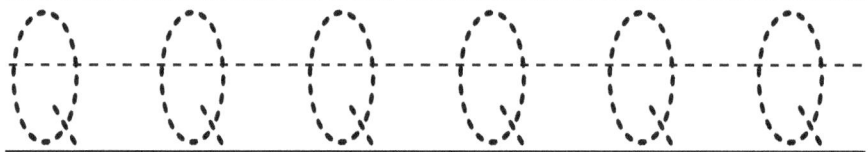

Q   Q   Q   Q   Q   Q   Q

Q   Q   Q   Q   Q   Q

Q

Q

Quintessential   Quintessential

You are Quintessential!

You are a quintessential hero to someone special.

Trace each letter and word. Practice writing each letter on your own.

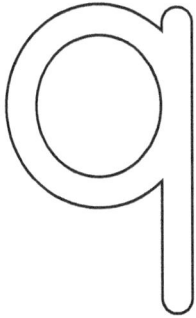

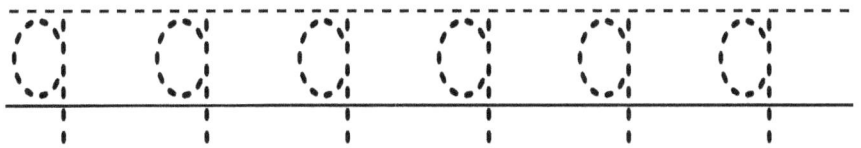

q   q   a   a   a   a   a

a   a   a   a   a   a

q

a

quintessential   quintessential

Be quintessential!

You are a quintessential hero to someone special.

You are
Quintessential!

Name:_____ Date:_____

Draw items that start with the letter in the box. You may also find pictures that start with the letter and paste the pictures here.

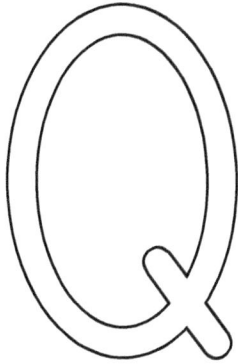

Q

Trace each letter and word. Practice writing each letter on your own.

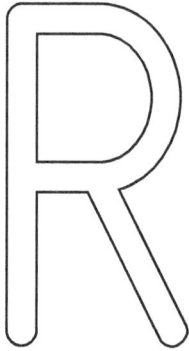

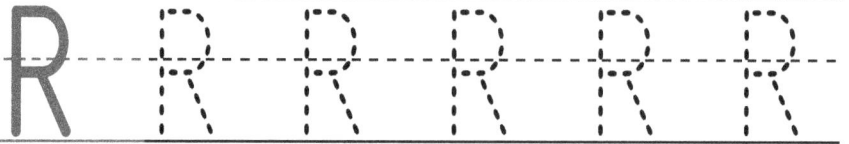

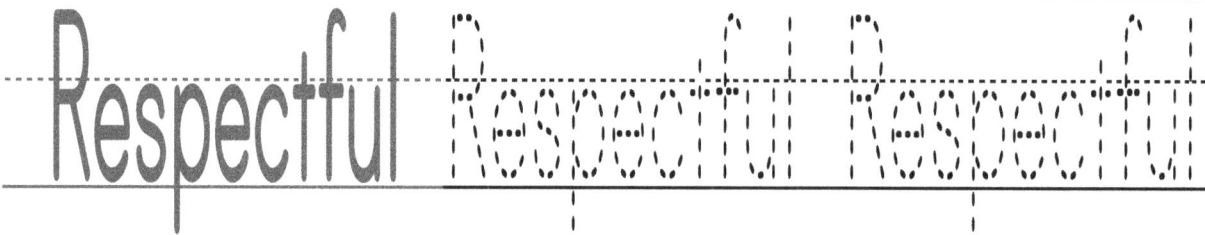

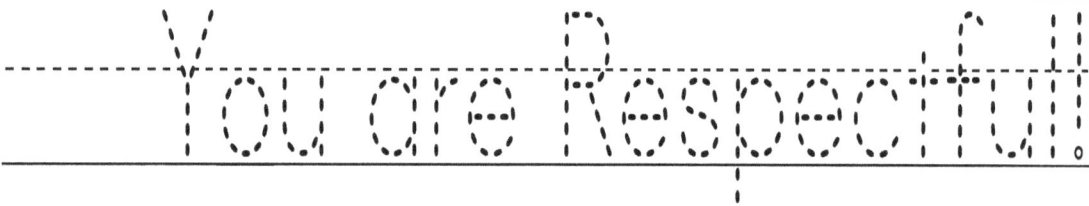

R   R R R R R R

R R R R R R R

R

R

Respectful Respectful Respectful

You are Respectful!

Being respectful will lead to endless possibilities.

Trace each letter and word. Practice writing each letter on your own.

r r r r r r r r r

r r r r r r r r r

r

r

respectful respectful

Be respectful!

Being respectful will lead to endless possibilities.

Be Respectful!

Name:_____ Date:_____

Draw items that start with the letter in the box. You may also find pictures that start with the letter and paste the pictures here.

R

Trace each letter and word. Practice writing each letter on your own.

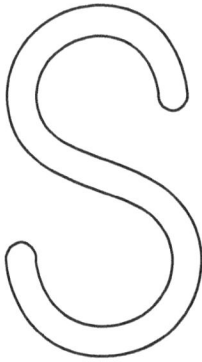

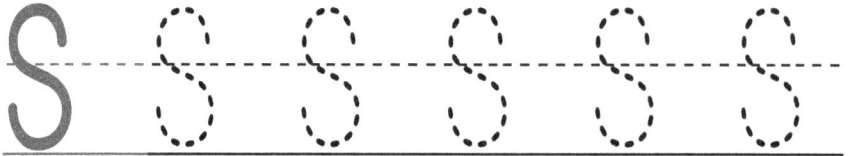

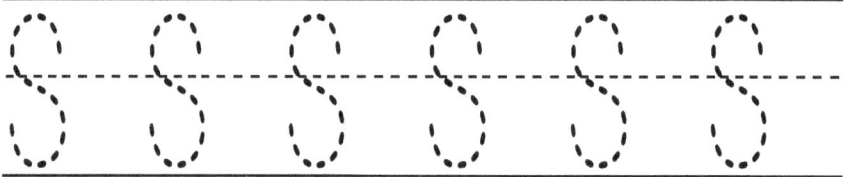

S

S S S S S S

S S S S S S

S

S

Special Special Special

You are Special!

Your spirit is a special kind of spirit.

Name:_____ Date:_____

Trace each letter and word. Practice writing each letter on your own.

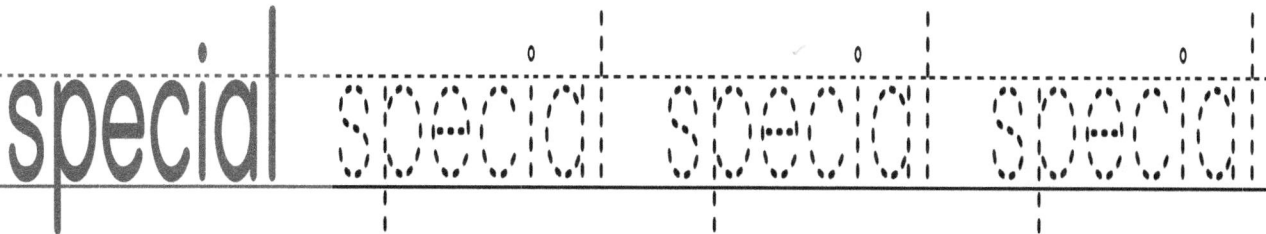

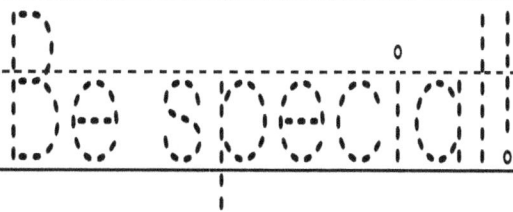

S   S s s s s s s s

s s s s s s s

s

s

special special special special

Be special!

Your spirit is a special kind of spirit.

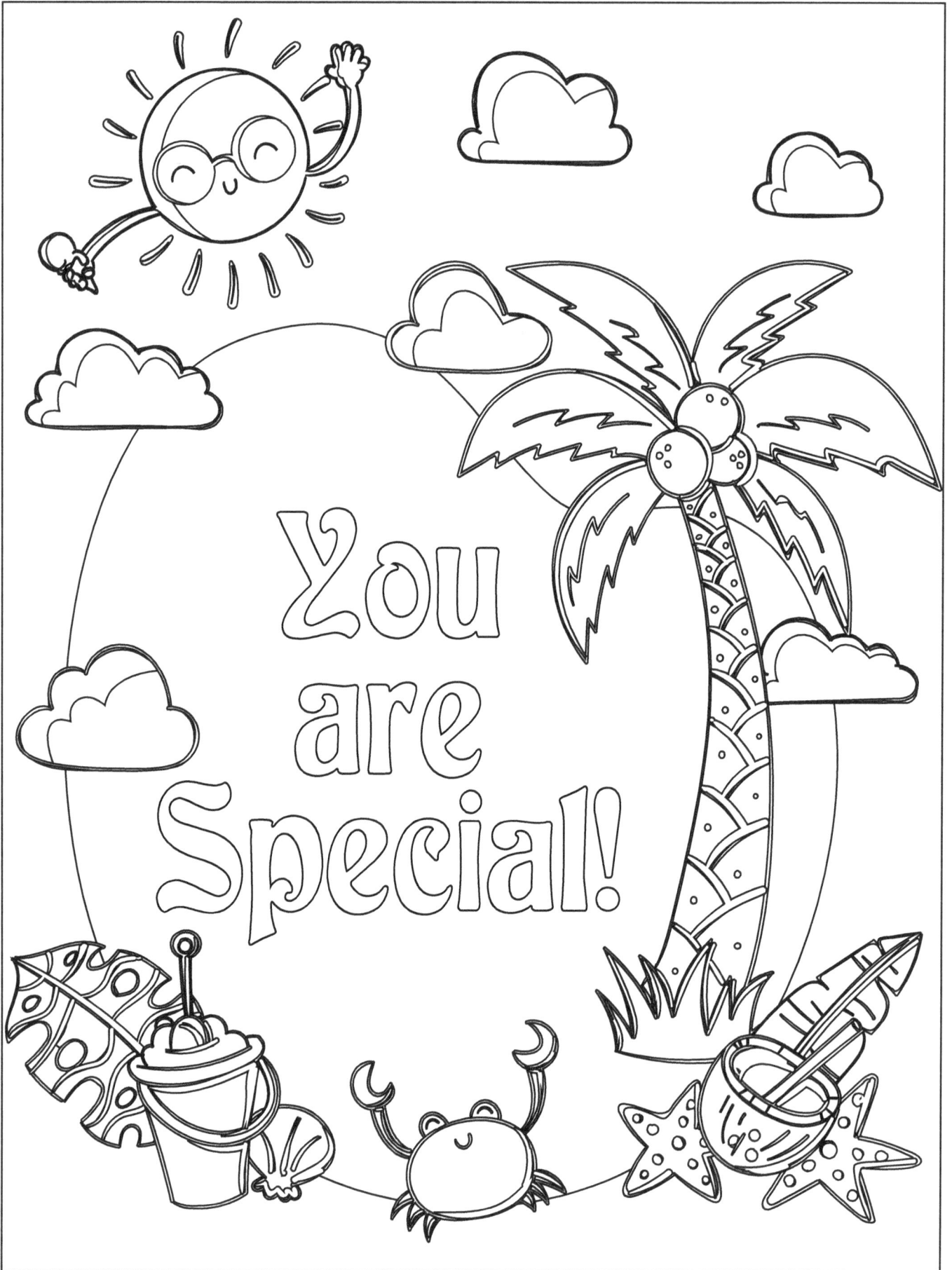

You are
Special!

Name:_____ Date:_____

Draw items that start with the letter in the box. You may also find pictures that start with the letter and paste the pictures here.

S

Trace each letter and word. Practice writing each letter on your own.

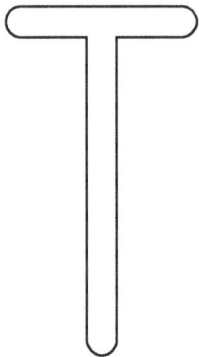

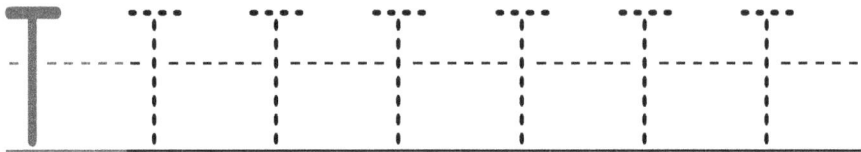

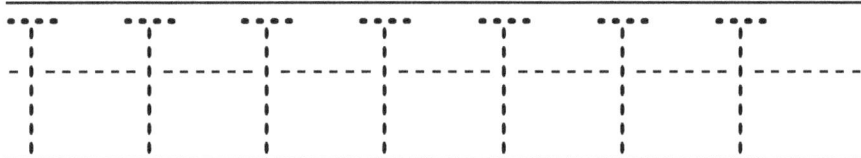

T

T T T T T T T T

T T T T T T T

T

T

Talented Talented Talented

You are Talented!

Let your talent lead you to living out your dreams.

Trace each letter and word. Practice writing each letter on your own.

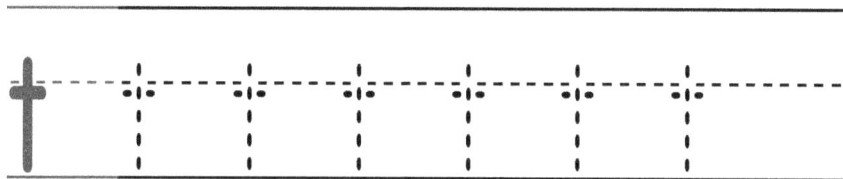

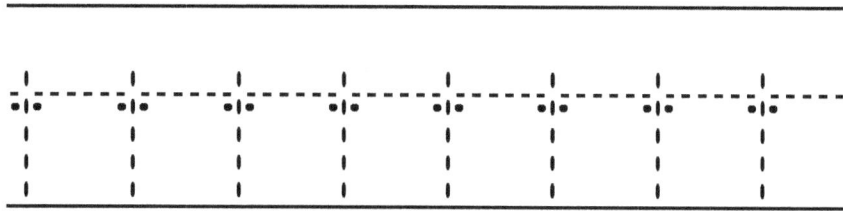

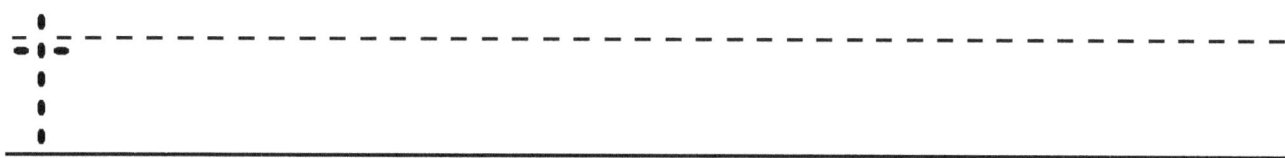

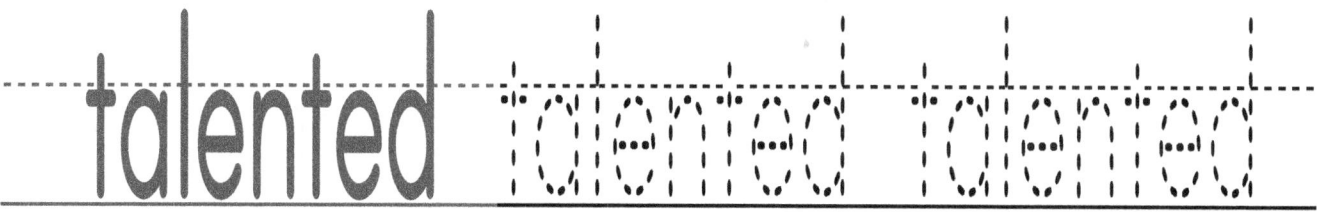

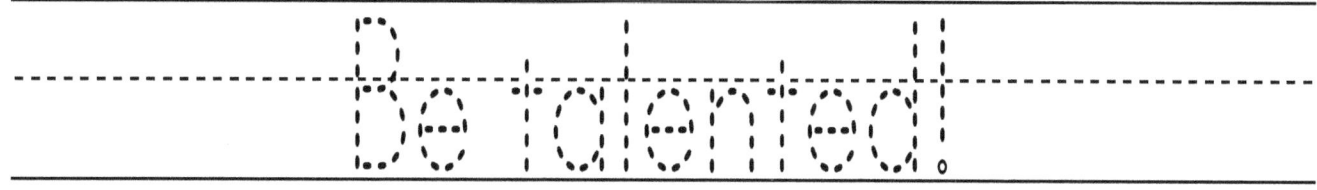

t

t t t t t t t

t t t t t t t t

t

t

talented talented talented

Be talented!

Let your talent lead you to living out your dreams.

BE TALENTED!

Name:_____ Date:_____

Draw items that start with the letter in the box. You may also find pictures that start with the letter and paste the pictures here.

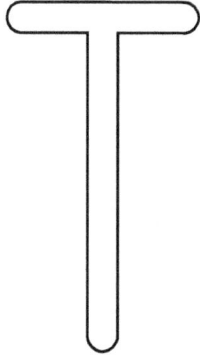

T

Name:_____ Date:_____

Trace each letter and word. Practice writing each letter on your own.

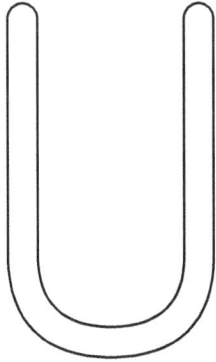

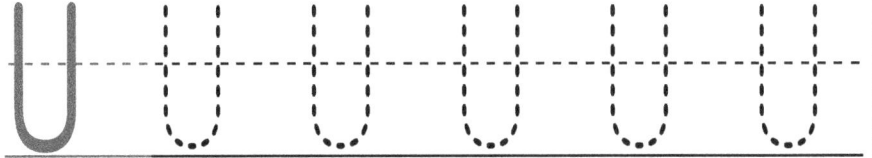

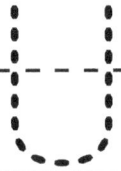

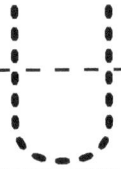

U   U U U U U U U U U U U U

U U U U U U U U U U U U

U

U

Unique Unique Unique

You are Unique!

Your life is unique, live your own journey in your own way.

Name:_____ Date:_____

Trace each letter and word. Practice writing each letter on your own.

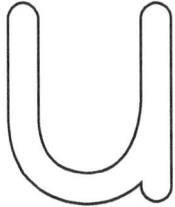

u u u u u u

u u u u u u

u

u

unique unique unique

Be unique!

Your life is unique, live your own journey in your own way.

YOU ARE UNIQUE!

Name:_____ Date:_____

Draw items that start with the letter in the box. You may also find pictures that start with the letter and paste the pictures here.

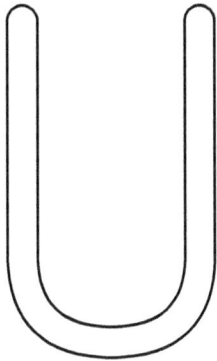

U

Trace each letter and word. Practice writing each letter on your own.

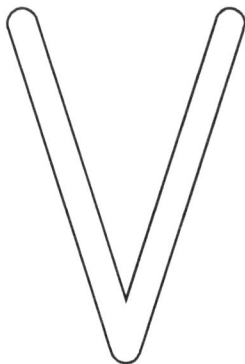

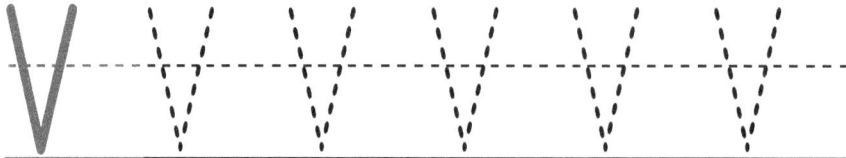

V

V v v v v v v v v
v v v v v v v v v

v

v

Victorious Victorious

You are Victorious!

You will be victorious in everything you do.

Name:_____ Date:_____

Trace each letter and word. Practice writing each letter on your own.

V   V   V   V   V   V   V

V   V   V   V   V   V

v

v

victorious victorious

Be victorious!

You will be victorious in everything you do.

BE VICTORIOUS!

Name:_____ Date:_____

Draw items that start with the letter in the box. You may also find pictures that start with the letter and paste the pictures here.

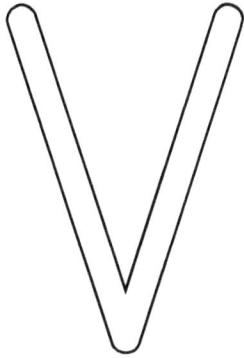

V

Name:_____ Date:_____

Trace each letter and word. Practice writing each letter on your own.

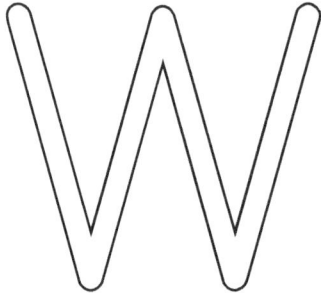

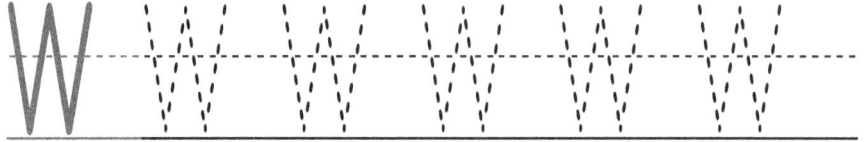

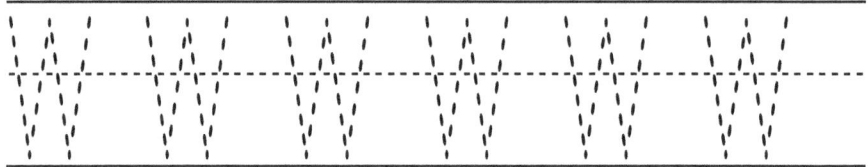

W

W   W W W W W

W W W W W W

W

W

Witty   Witty   Witty

You are Witty!

Show off your witty and charming personality.

Name:_____   Date:_____

Trace each letter and word. Practice writing each letter on your own.

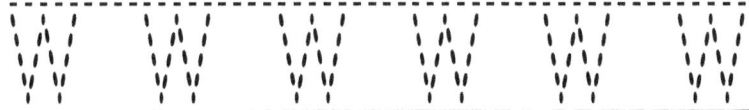

W   W   W   W   W   W

W   W   W   W   W   W

W

W

witty   witty   witty

Be witty!

Show off your witty and charming personality.

YOU ARE WITTY!

Name:_____ Date:_____

Draw items that start with the letter in the box. You may also find pictures that start with the letter and paste the pictures here.

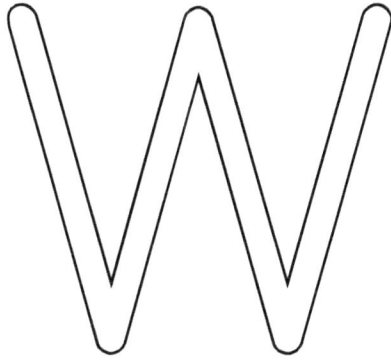

W

Trace each letter and word. Practice writing each letter on your own.

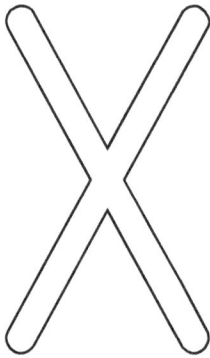

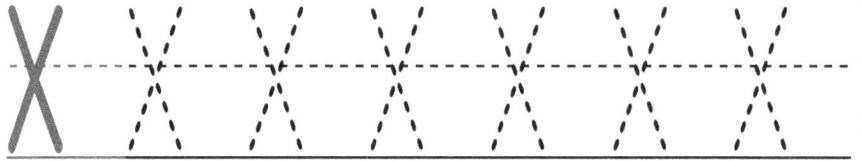

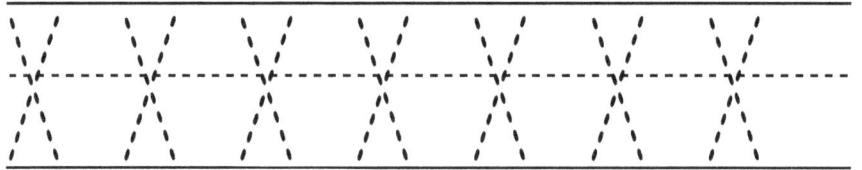

X   X X X X X X X X

X X X X X X X X

X

X

X-factor X-factor

You are a X-factor!

You have that X-factor that makes you extraordinary.

Trace each letter and word. Practice writing each letter on your own.

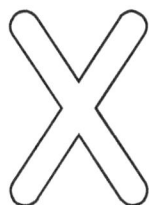

X   X   X   X   X   X   X   X   X

X   X   X   X   X   X   X   X   X

x

x

x-factor x-factor

Be the x-factor!

You have that X-factor that makes you extraordinary.

Be the X-Factor!

Name:_____ Date:_____

Draw items that start with the letter in the box. You may also find pictures that start with the letter and paste the pictures here.

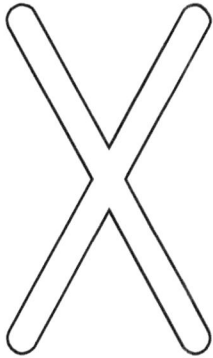

X

Name:_____ Date:_____

Trace each letter and word. Practice writing each letter on your own.

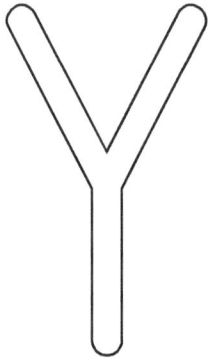

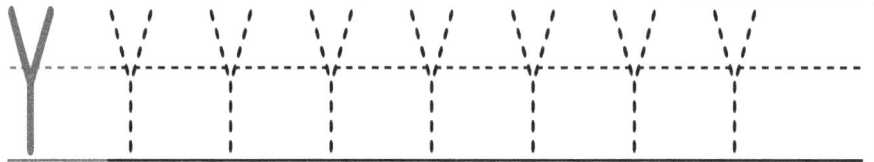

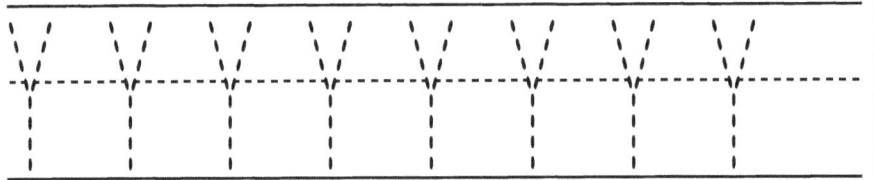

Y

Y Y Y Y Y Y Y Y Y Y

Y Y Y Y Y Y Y Y Y

Y

Y

Youthful Youthful

You are Youthful!

The youthful side of you should live on forever.

Trace each letter and word. Practice writing each letter on your own.

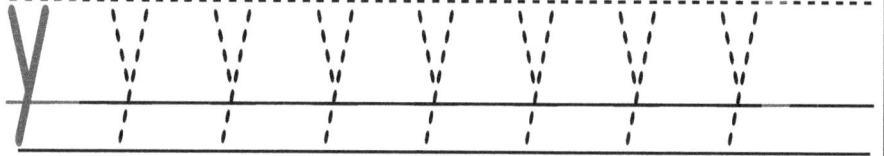

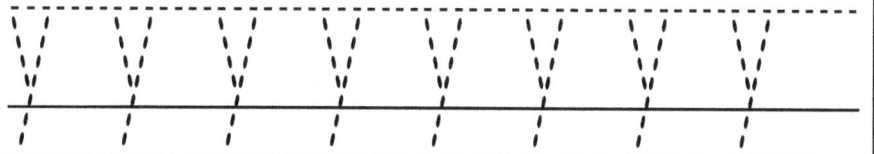

y

y y y y y y y y y

y y y y y y y y y

y

y

youthful youthful

Be youthful!

The youthful side of you should live on forever.

You are Youthful!

Name:_____ Date:_____

Draw items that start with the letter in the box. You may also find pictures that start with the letter and paste the pictures here.

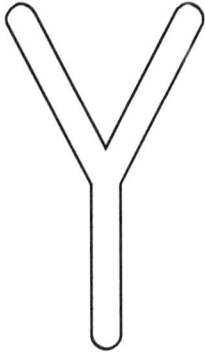

Y

Trace each letter and word. Practice writing each letter on your own.

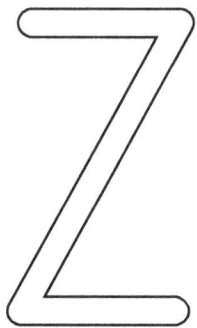

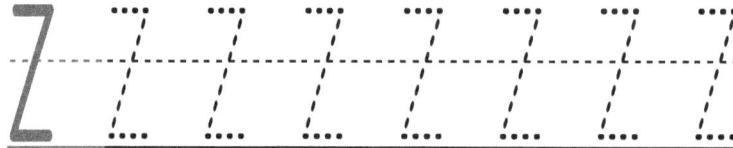

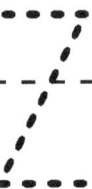

Z

Z Z Z Z Z Z Z Z Z

Z Z Z Z Z Z Z Z

Z

Z

Zestful Zestful Zestful

You are Zestful!

Your zestful personality charms all whom cross your path.

Name:_____ Date:_____

Trace each letter and word. Practice writing each letter on your own.

Z

Z Z Z Z Z Z Z Z Z

Z Z Z Z Z Z Z Z Z

Z

Z

zestful zestful zestful

Be zestful

Your zestful personality charms all whom cross your path.

Be Zestful!

Name:_____ Date:_____

Draw items that start with the letter in the box. You may also find pictures that start with the letter and paste the pictures here.

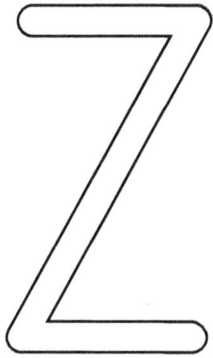

Z

Extra Handwriting
Practice Sheets

Name:_____ Date:_____

Trace each letter. Practice writing each letter on your own.

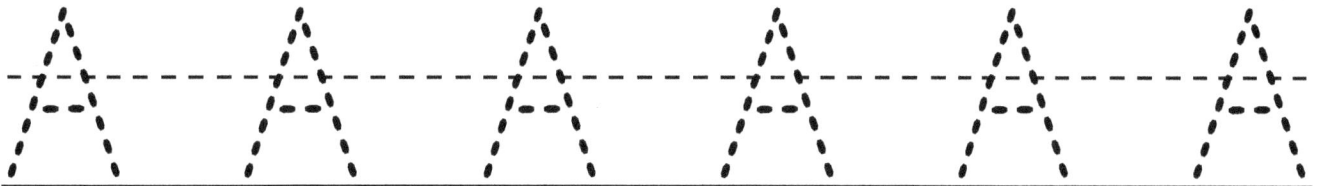

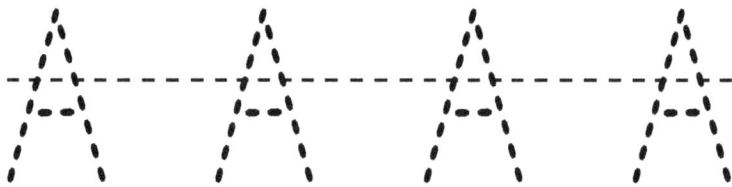

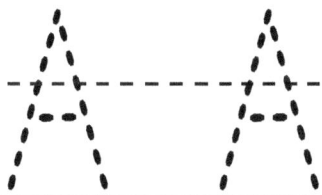

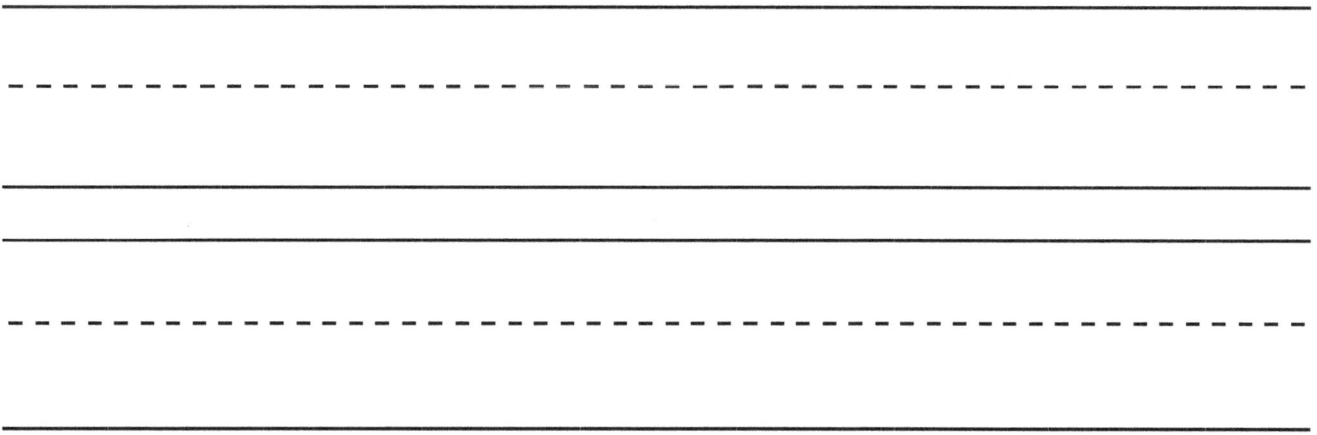

A A A A A A

A A A A

A A A

A A

A

Trace each letter. Practice writing each letter on your own.

a a a a a a

a a a a

a a a

a a

a

Name:_____ Date:_____

Trace each letter. Practice writing each letter on your own.

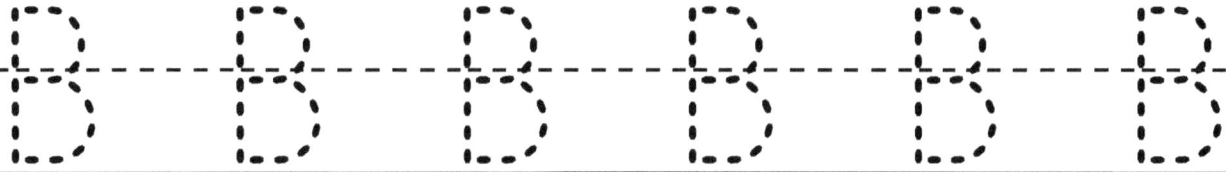

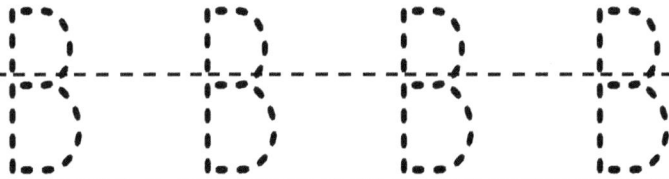

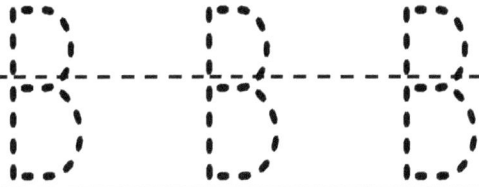

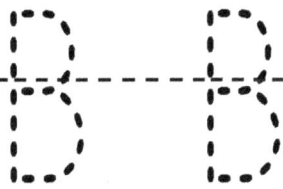

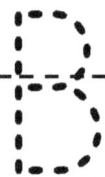

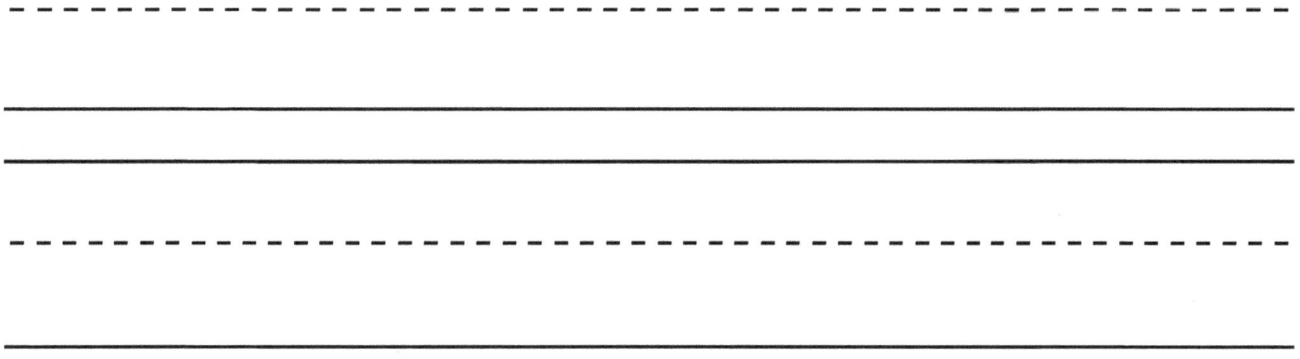

B   B   B   B   B   B

B   B   B   B

B   B   B

B   B

B

Trace each letter. Practice writing each letter on your own.

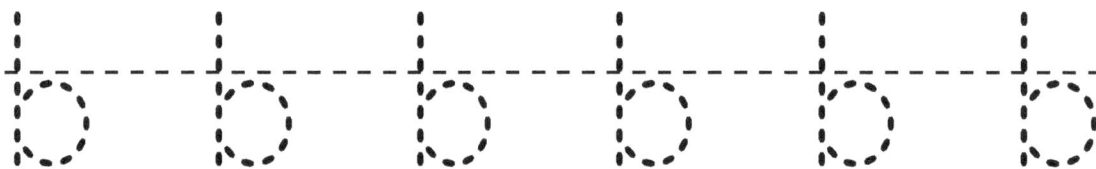

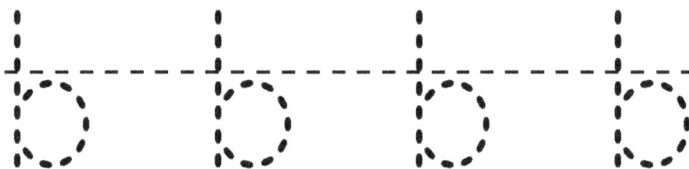

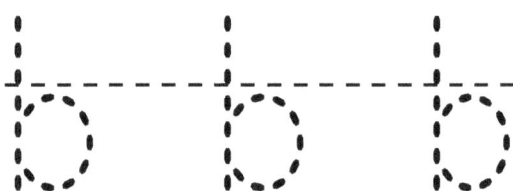

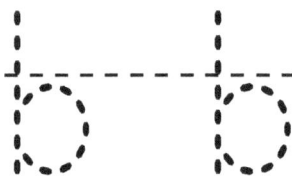

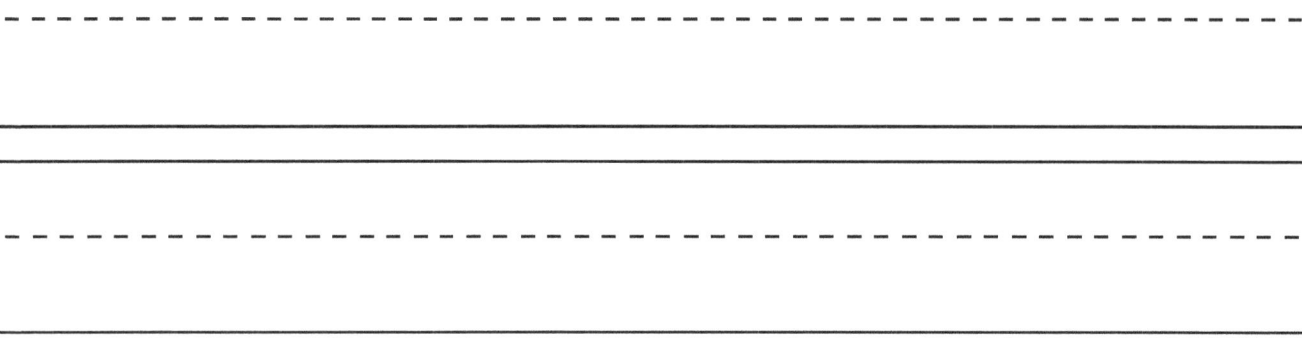

b b b b b b

b b b b

b b b

b b

b

Trace each letter. Practice writing each letter on your own.

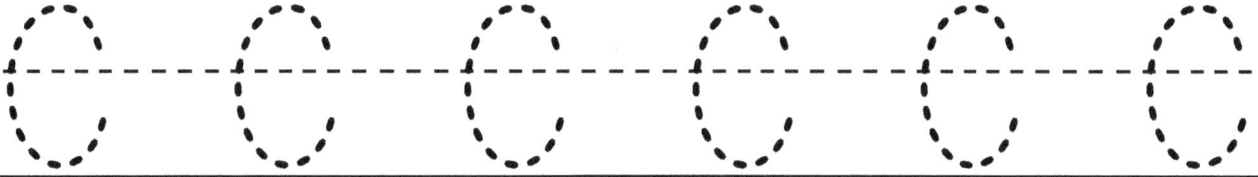

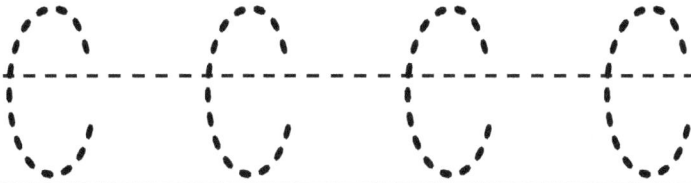

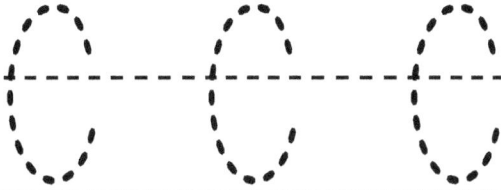

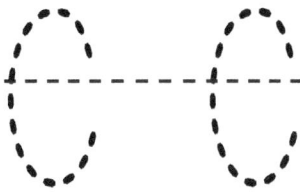

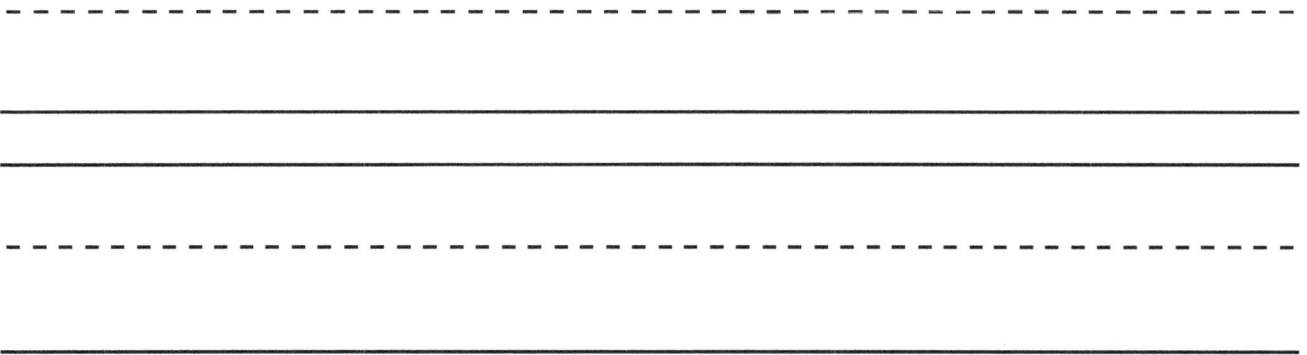

C C C C C C

C C C C

C C C

C C

C

Trace each letter. Practice writing each letter on your own.

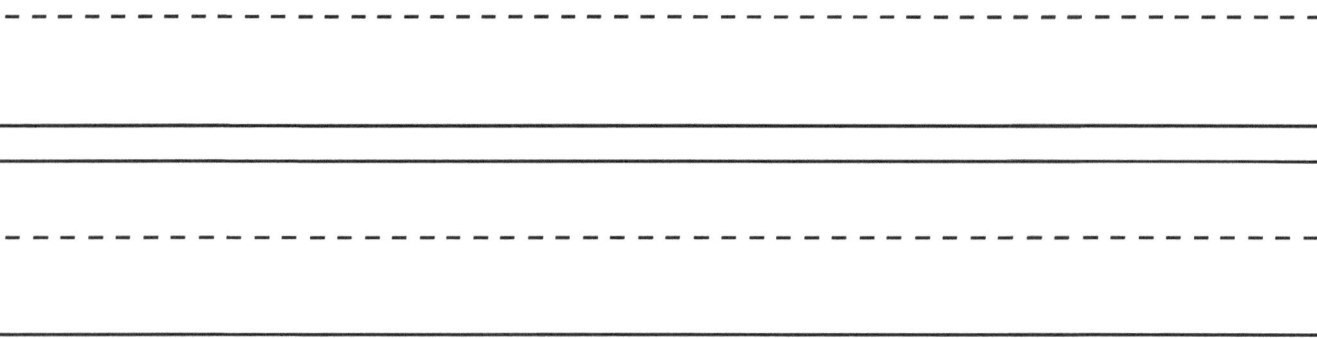

C C C C C C C

C C C C

C C C

C C

C

Name:_____ Date:_____

Trace each letter. Practice writing each letter on your own.

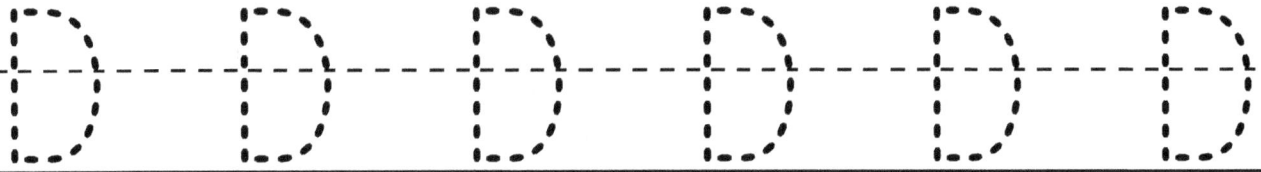

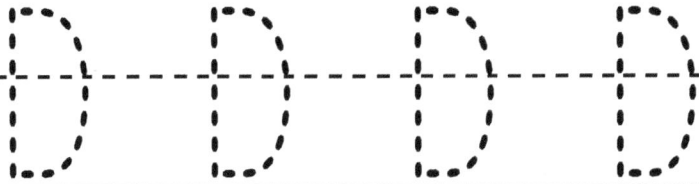

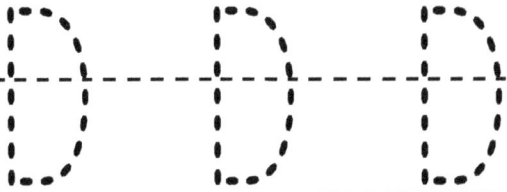

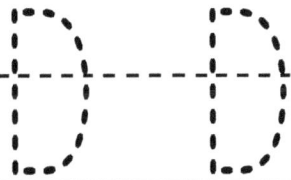

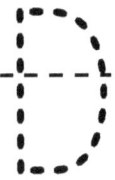

D   D   D   D   D   D

D   D   D   D

D   D   D

D   D

D

Name:_____ Date:_____

Trace each letter. Practice writing each letter on your own.

d d d d d d d

d d d d

d d d

d d

d

Trace each letter. Practice writing each letter on your own.

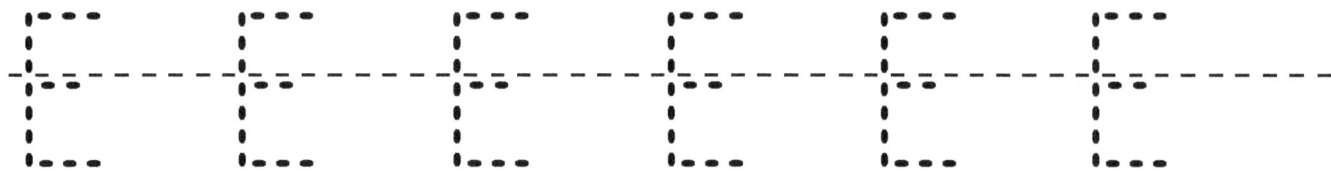

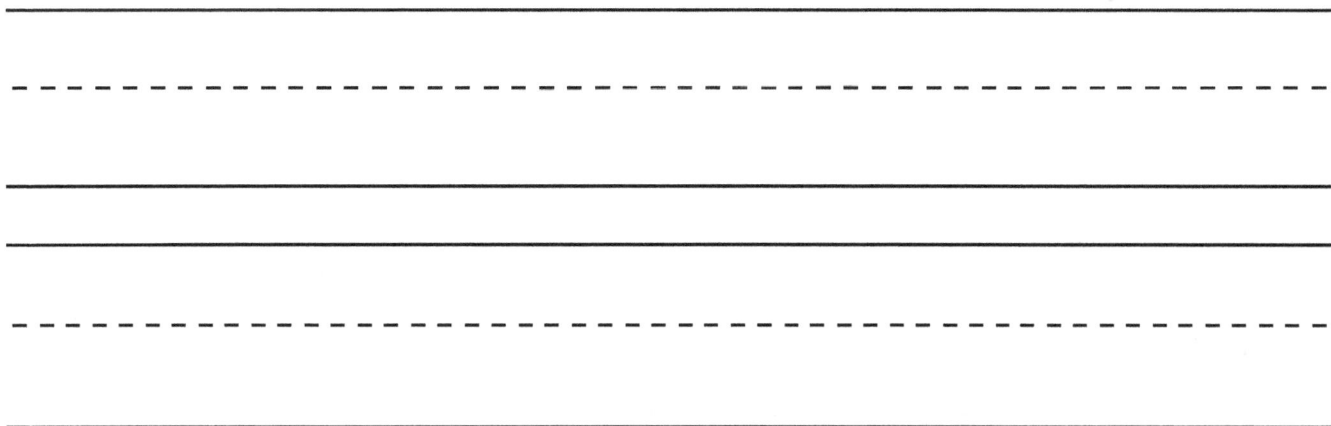

E E E E E

E E E E

E E E

E E

E

Trace each letter. Practice writing each letter on your own.

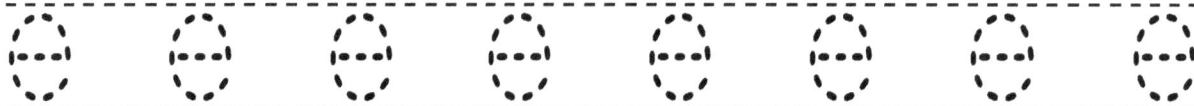

Name:_____ Date:_____

Trace each letter. Practice writing each letter on your own.

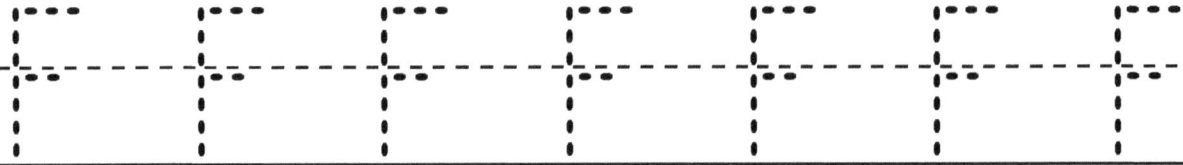

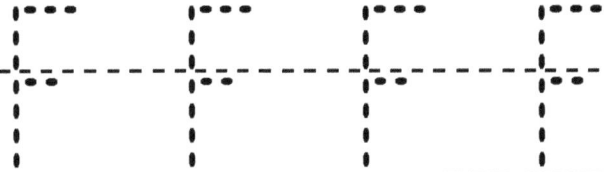

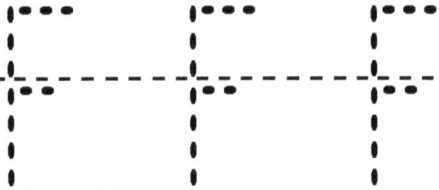

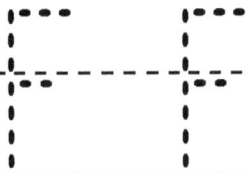

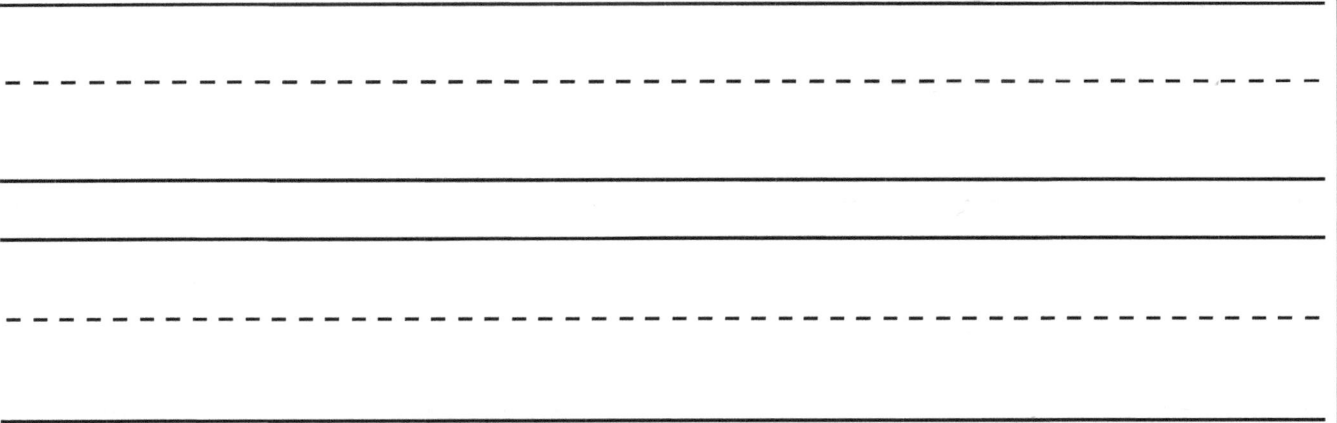

F F F F F F

F F F F

F F F

F F

F

Trace each letter. Practice writing each letter on your own.

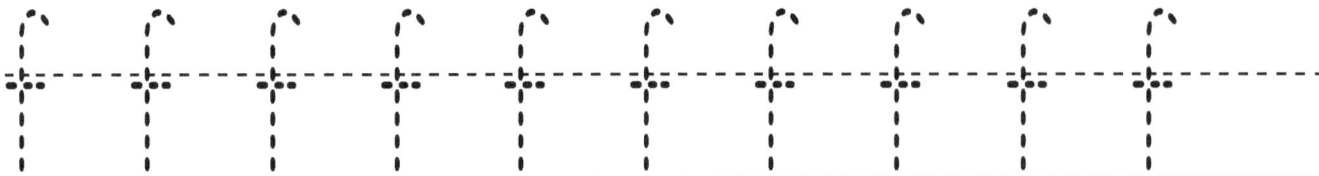

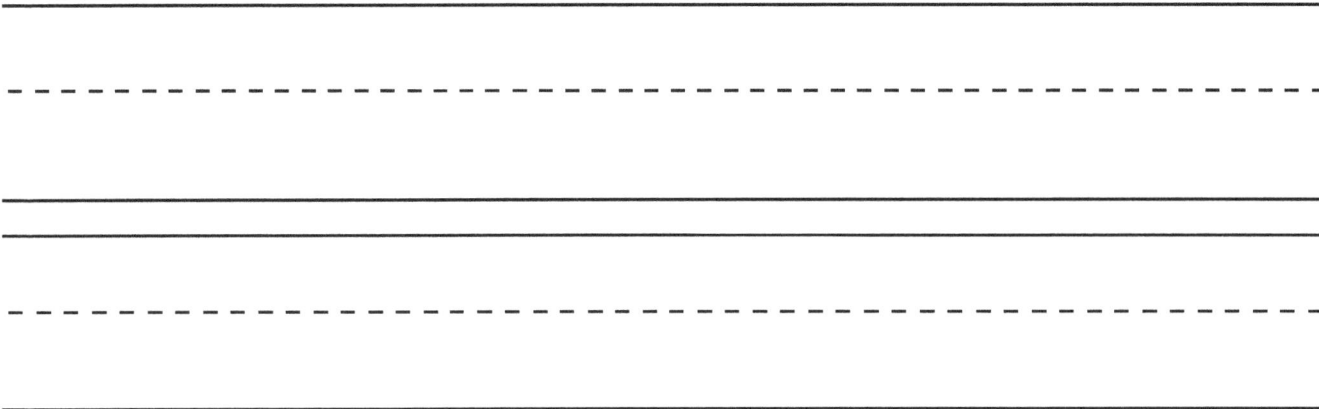

f f f f f f f f f f

f f f f

f f f

f f

f

Name:_____ Date:_____

Trace each letter. Practice writing each letter on your own.

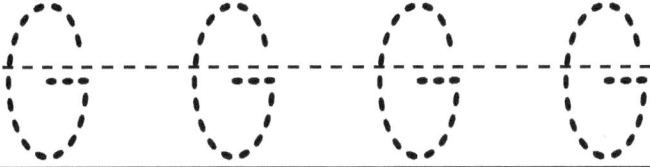

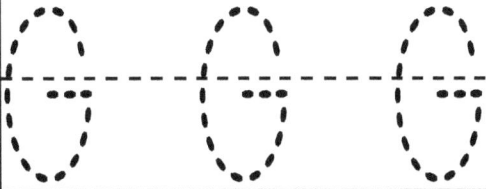

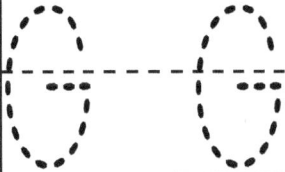

Name:_____ Date:_____

Trace each letter. Practice writing each letter on your own.

g g g g g g g g g

g g g g

g g g

g g

g

Name:_____ Date:_____

Trace each letter. Practice writing each letter on your own.

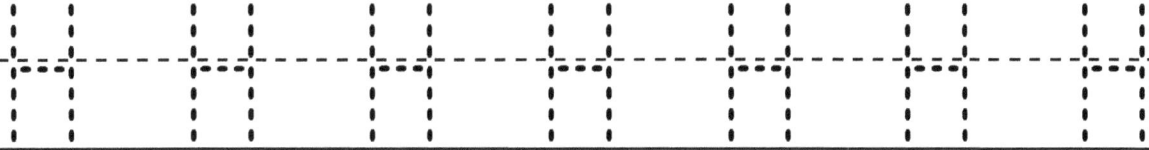

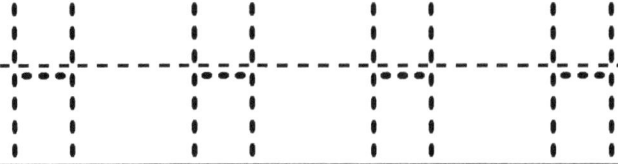

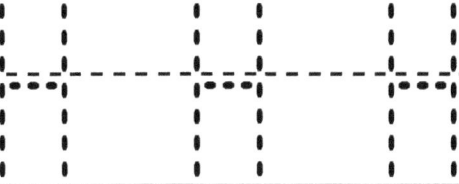

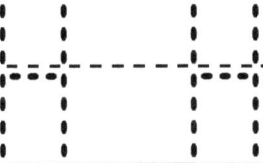

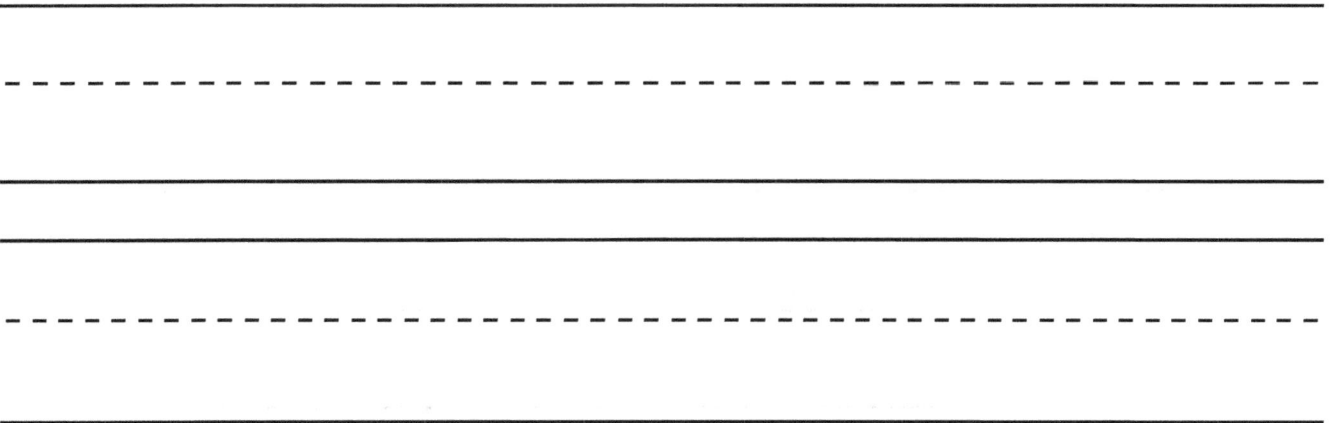

H H H H H H H

H H H H

H H H

H H

H

Name:_____ Date:_____

Trace each letter. Practice writing each letter on your own.

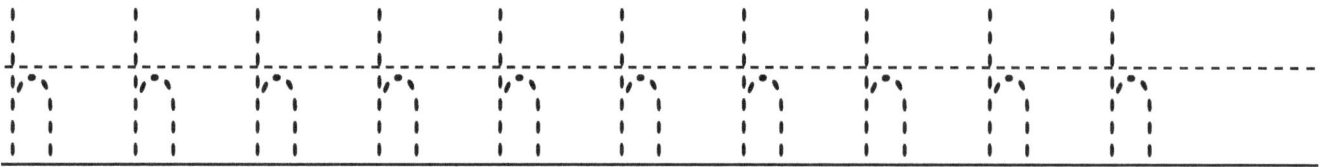

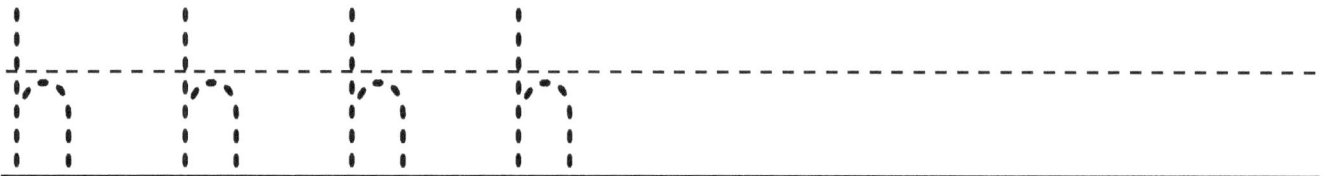

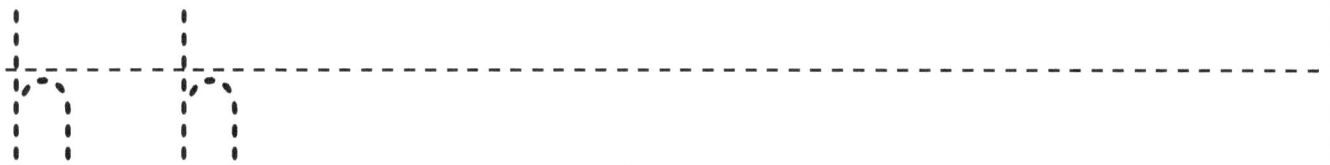

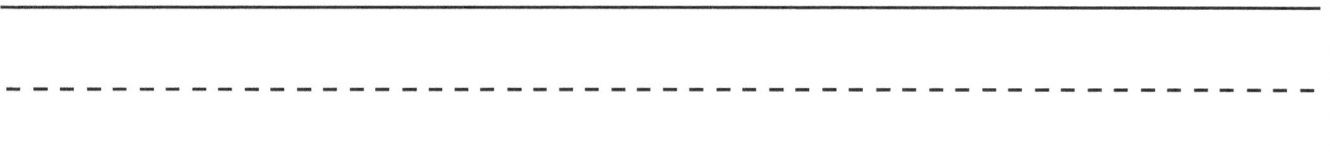

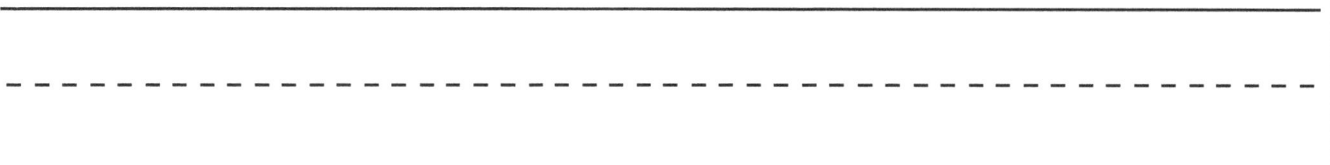

h h h h h h h h h h

h h h h

h h h

h h

h

Name:_____ Date:_____

Trace each letter. Practice writing each letter on your own.

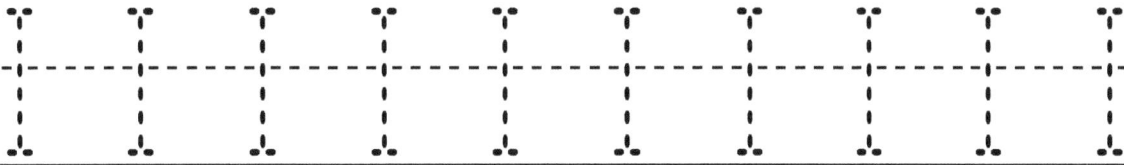

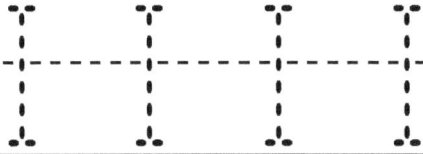

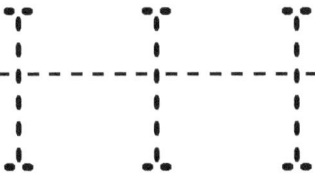

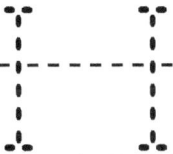

I I I I I I I I I I

I I I I

I I I

I I

I

Name:_____ Date:_____

Trace each letter. Practice writing each letter on your own.

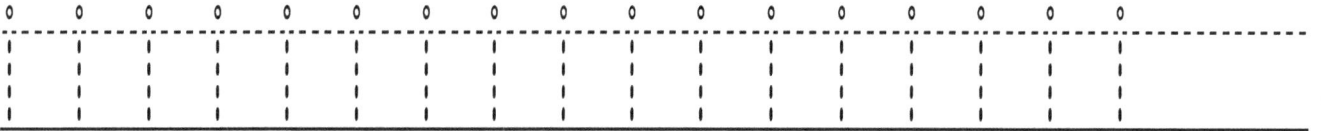

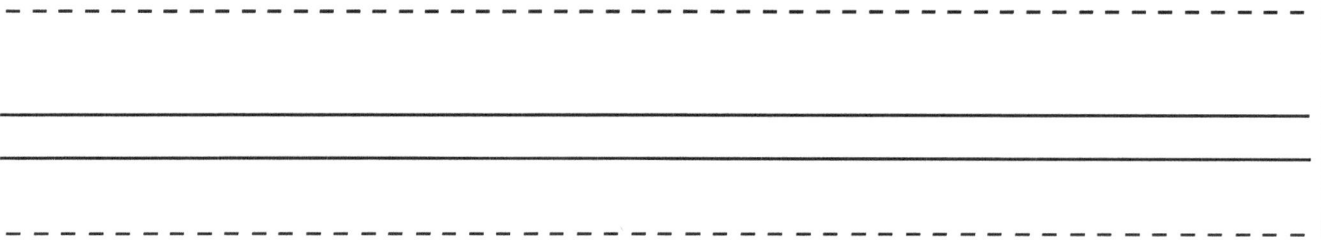

Name:_____ Date:_____

Trace each letter. Practice writing each letter on your own.

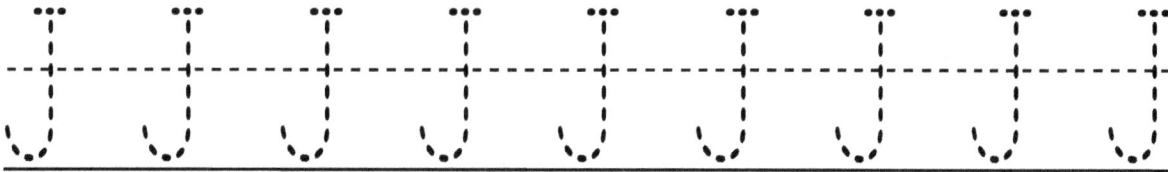

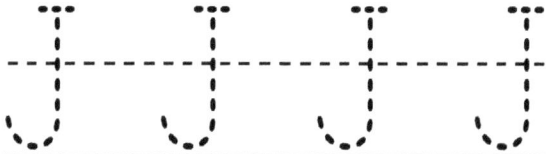

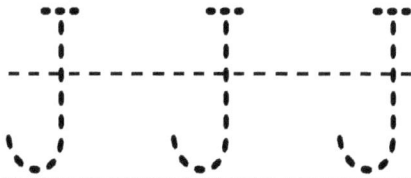

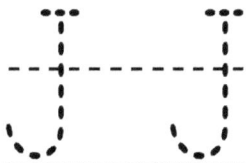

J J J J J J J J J

J J J J

J J J

J J

J

Trace each letter. Practice writing each letter on your own.

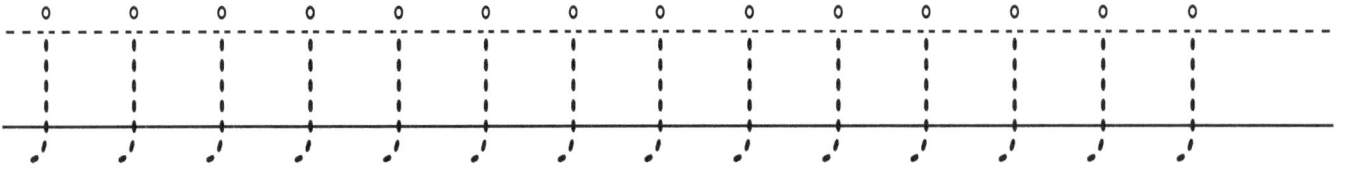

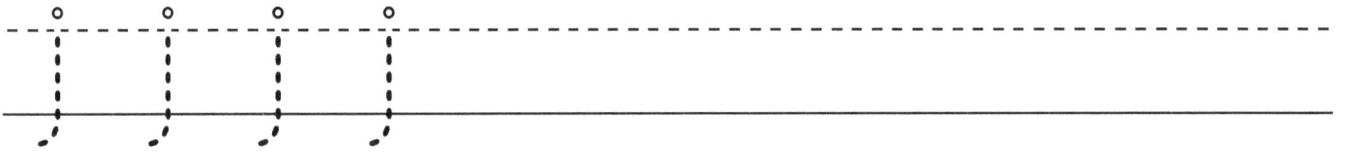

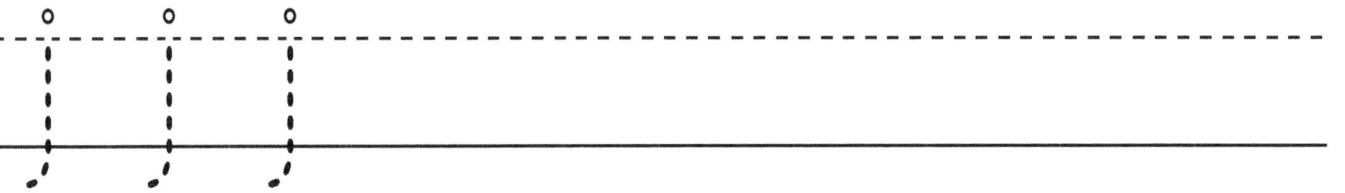

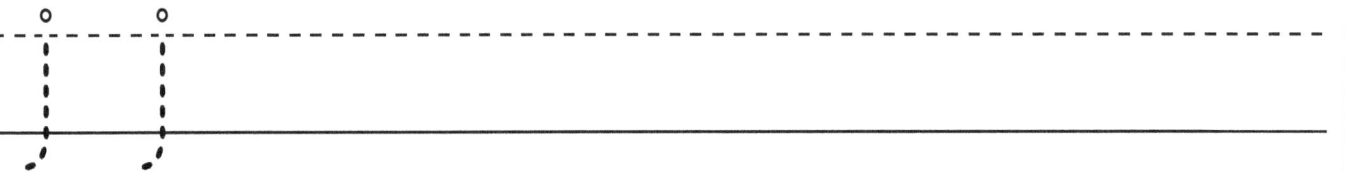

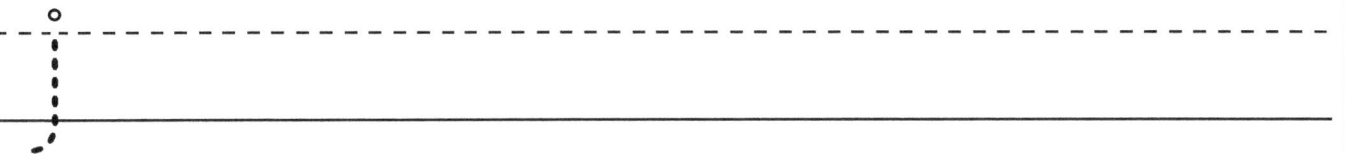

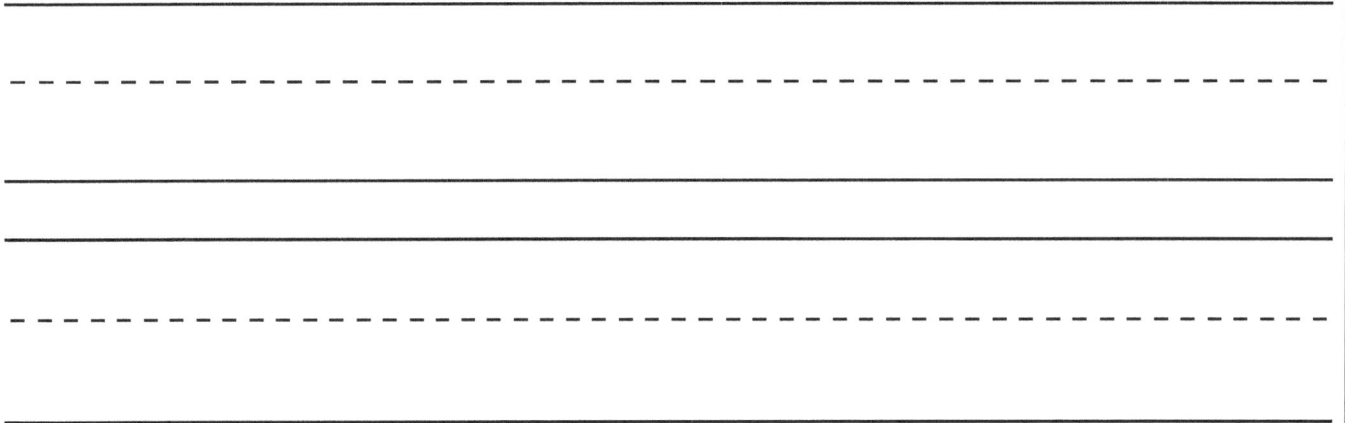

j j j j j j j j j j j j j j j

j j j j

j j j

j j

j

Name:_____ Date:_____

Trace each letter. Practice writing each letter on your own.

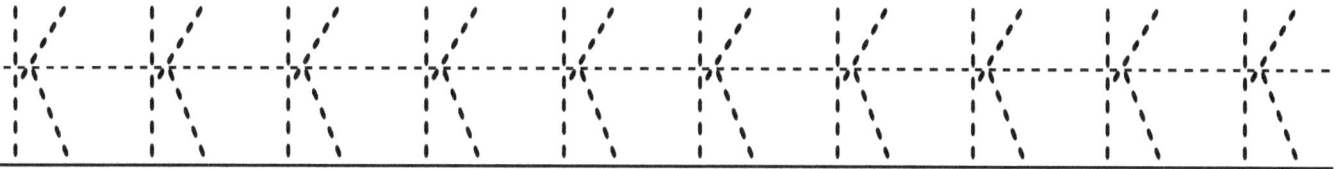

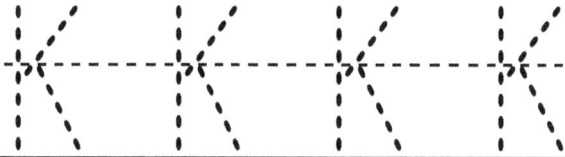

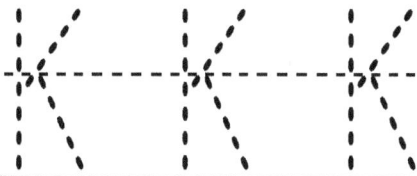

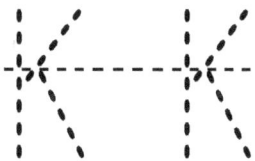

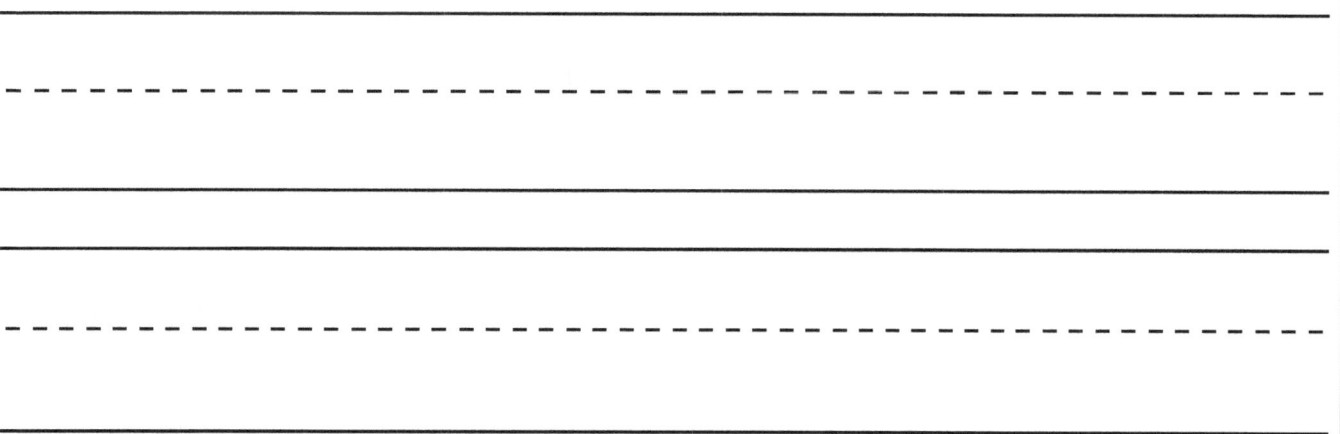

K K K K K K K K K K

K K K K

K K K

K K

K

Name:_____ Date:_____

Trace each letter. Practice writing each letter on your own.

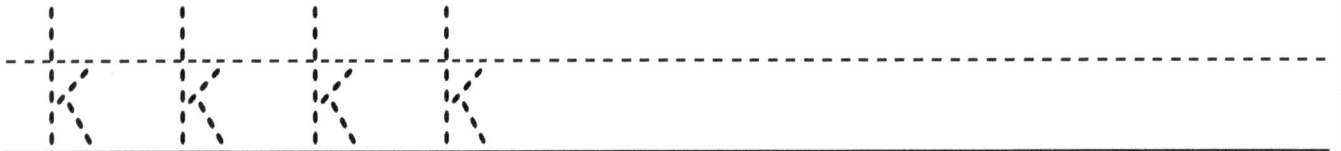

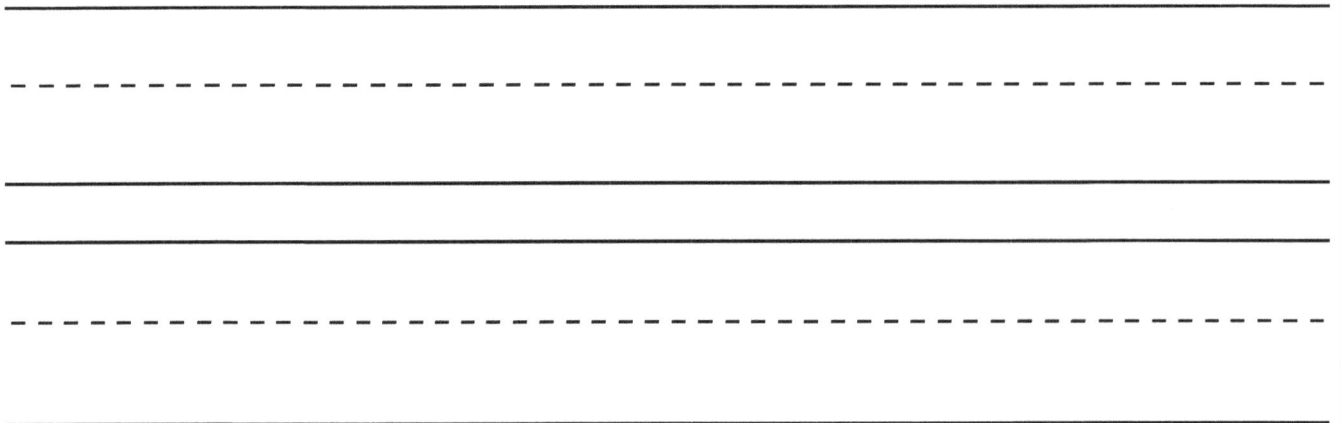

k k k k k k k k k k k k

k k k k

k k k

k k

k

Trace each letter. Practice writing each letter on your own.

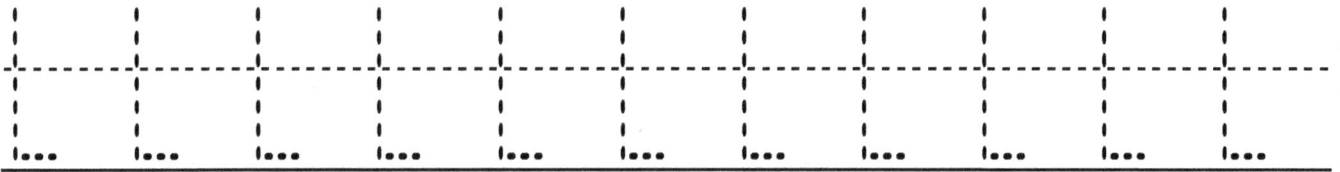

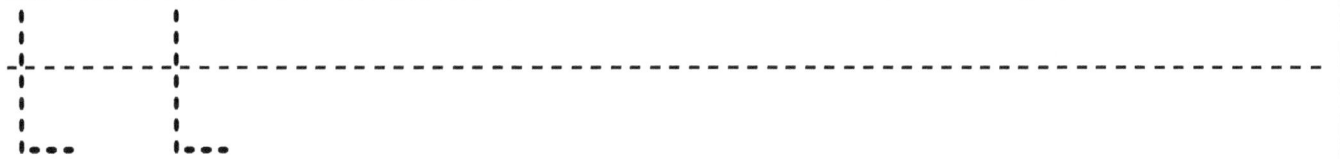

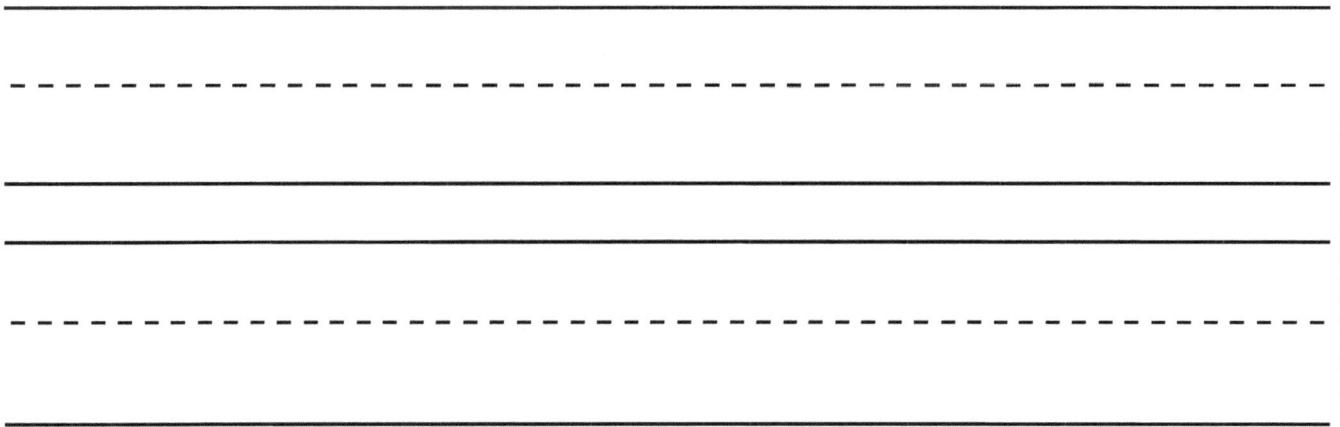

Name:_____ Date:_____

Trace each letter. Practice writing each letter on your own.

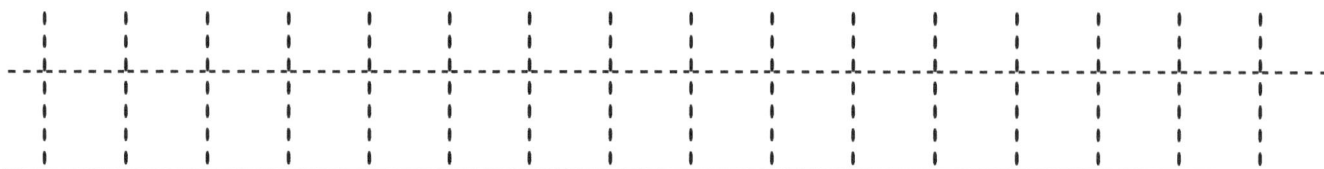

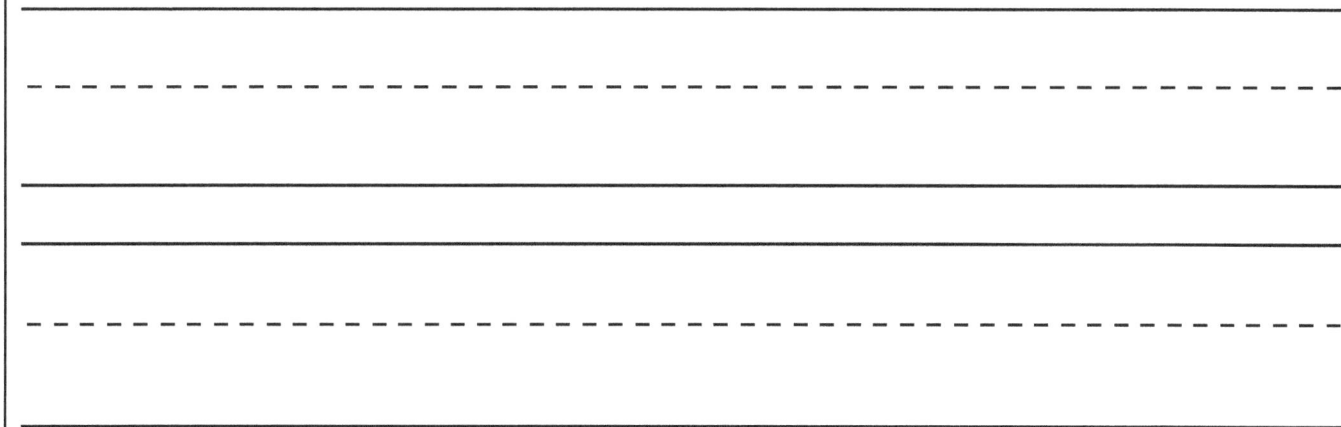

Trace each letter. Practice writing each letter on your own.

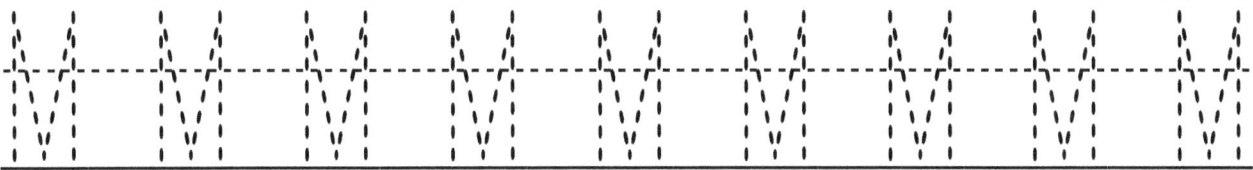

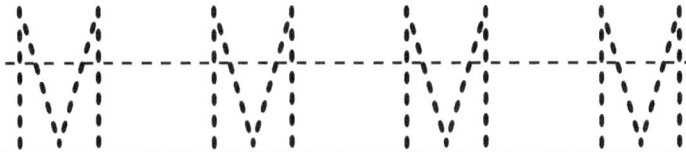

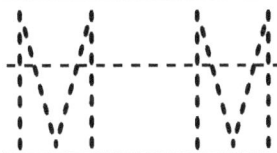

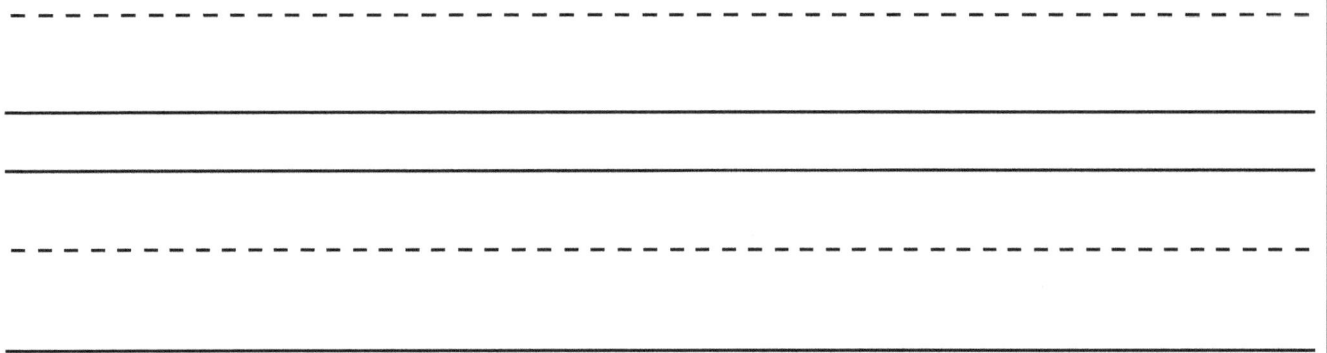

M M M M M M M M M M

M M M M

M M M

M M

M

Trace each letter. Practice writing each letter on your own.

m m m m m m m m m

m m m m

m m m

m m

m

Trace each letter. Practice writing each letter on your own.

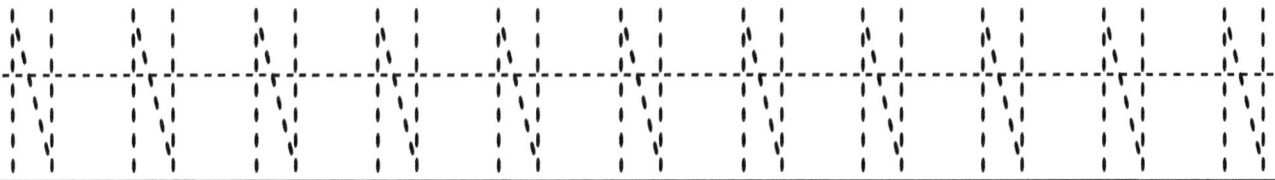

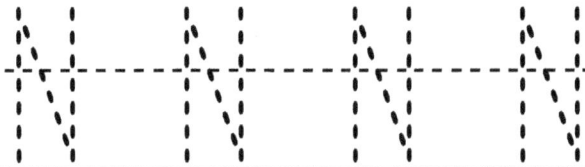

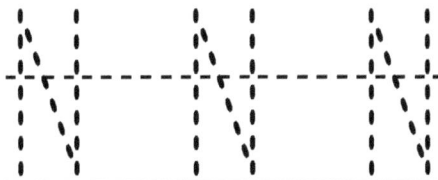

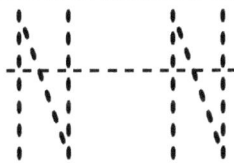

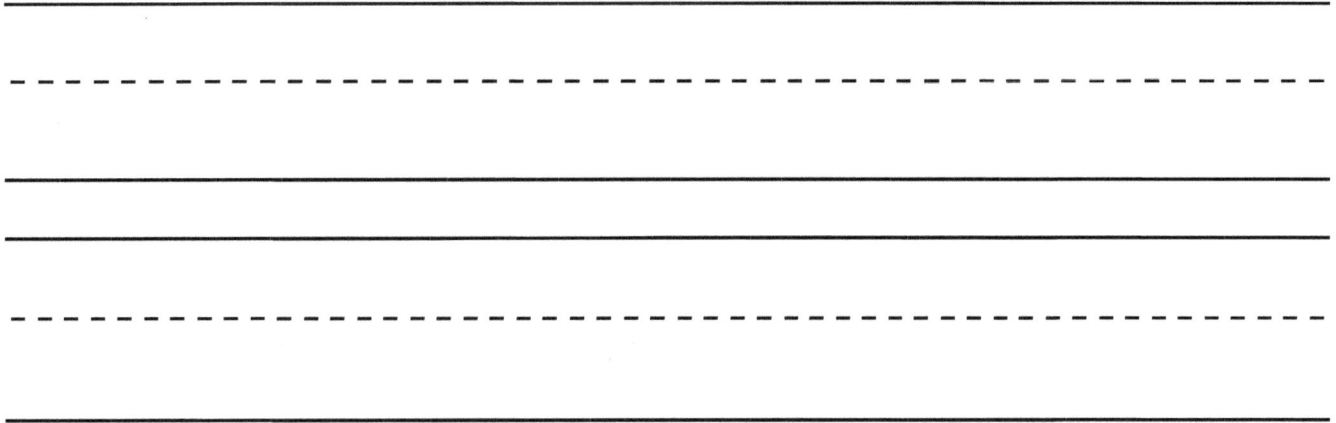

N N N N N N N N N N

N N N N

N N N

N N

N

Trace each letter. Practice writing each letter on your own.

n n n n n n n n n n n

n n n n

n n n

n n

n

Trace each letter. Practice writing each letter on your own.

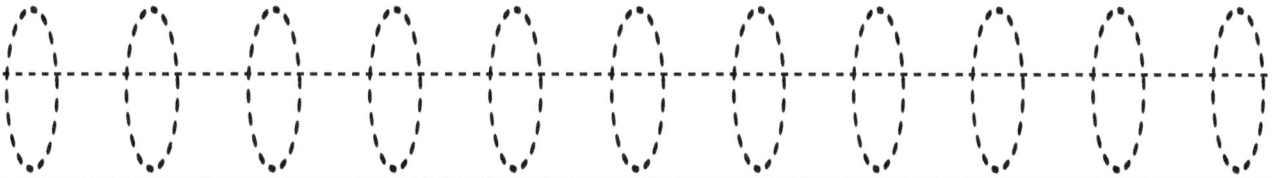

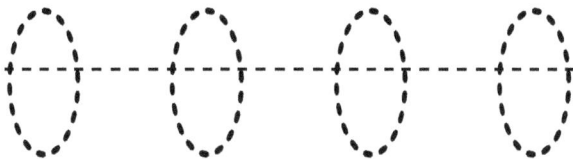

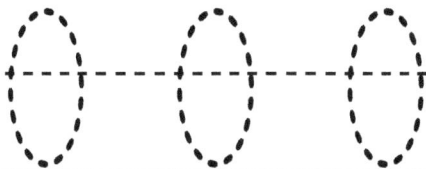

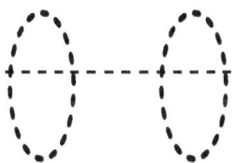

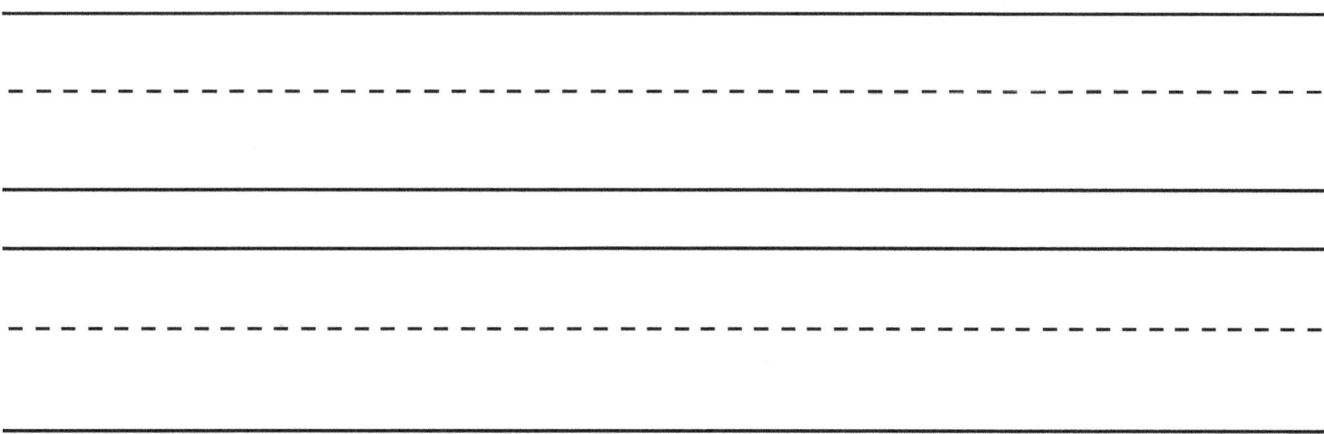

Name:_____ Date:_____

Trace each letter. Practice writing each letter on your own.

O O O O O O O O O O O O O O

O O O O

O O O

O O

O

Name:_____ Date:_____

Trace each letter. Practice writing each letter on your own.

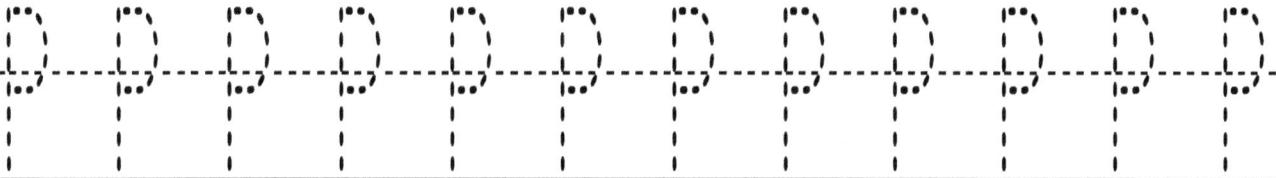

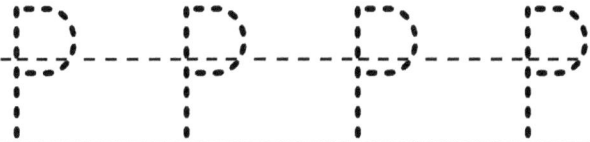

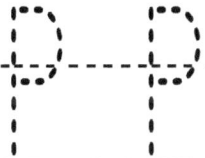

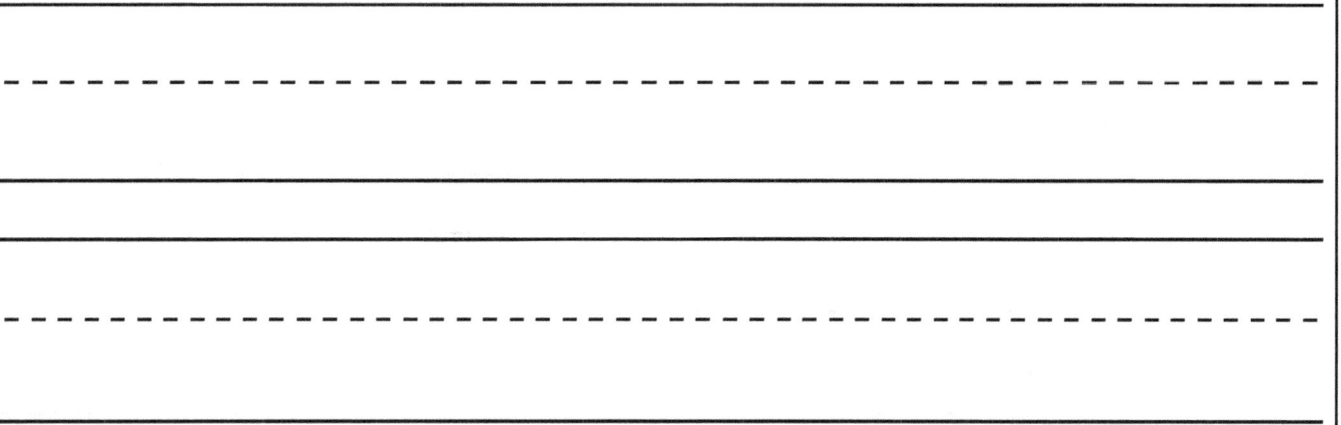

P P P P P P P P P P P P

P P P P

P P P

P P

P

Name:_____ Date:_____

Trace each letter. Practice writing each letter on your own.

p p p p p p p p p p p p p p

p p p p

p p p

p p

p

Trace each letter. Practice writing each letter on your own.

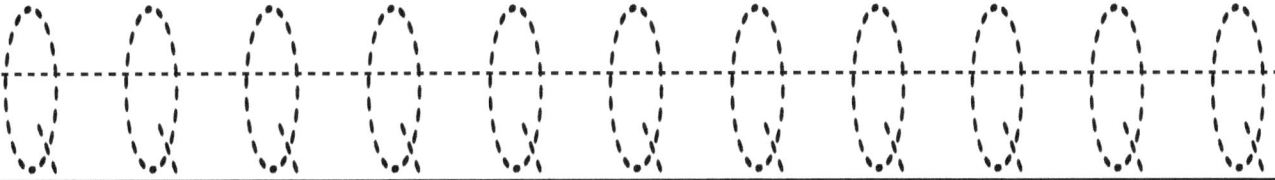

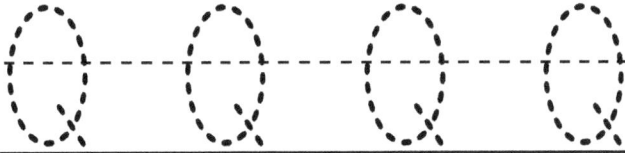

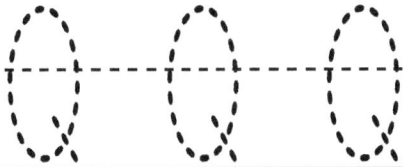

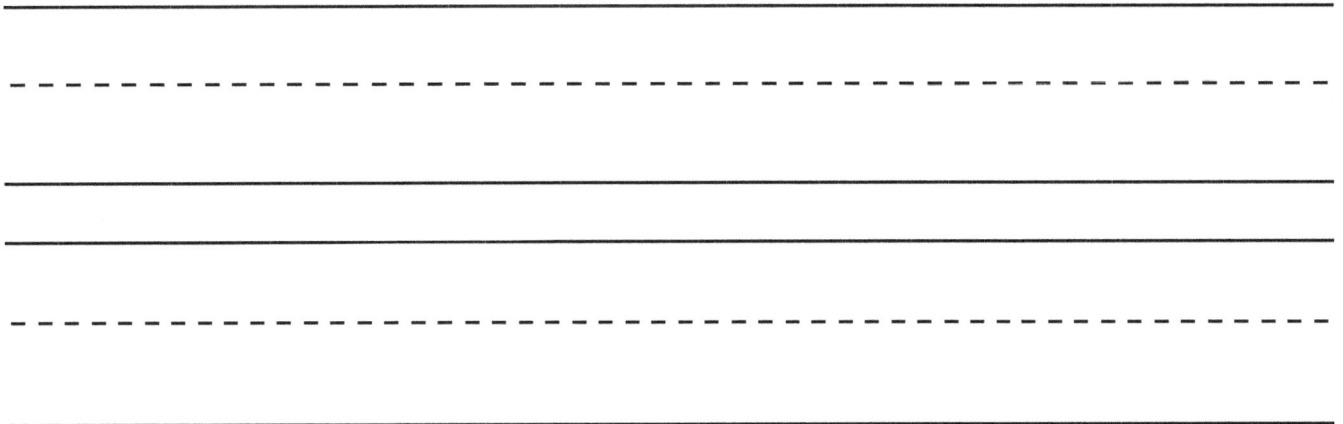

Q Q Q Q Q Q Q Q Q Q Q

Q Q Q Q

Q Q Q

Q

Q

Name:_____ Date:_____

Trace each letter. Practice writing each letter on your own.

a a a a a a a a a a a a a a

a a a a

a a a

a a

a

Trace each letter. Practice writing each letter on your own.

R R R R R R R R R R R R R

R R R R

R R R

R

R

Trace each letter. Practice writing each letter on your own.

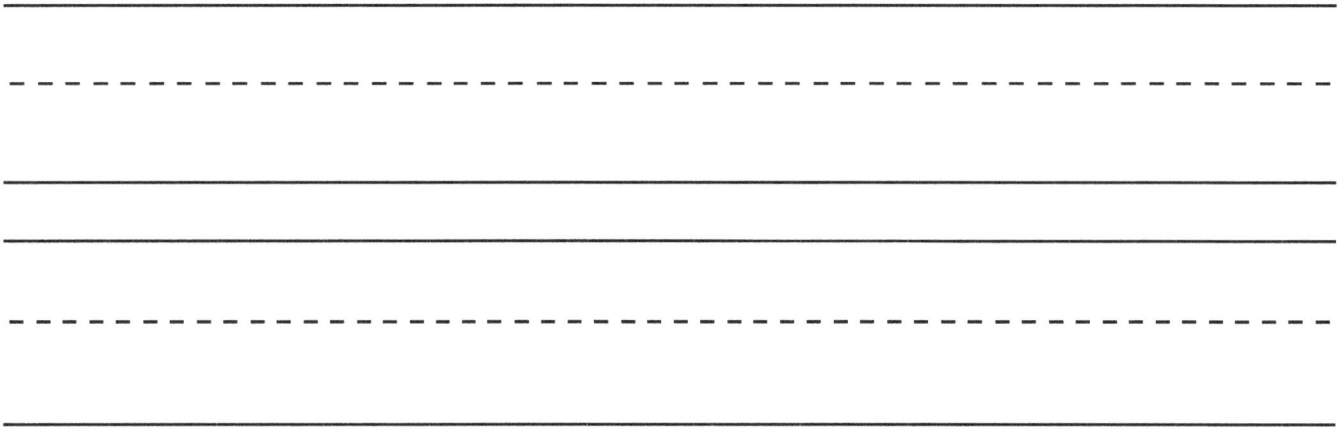

r r r r r r r r r r r r r r r

r r r r

r r r

r r

r

Name:_____ Date:_____

Trace each letter. Practice writing each letter on your own.

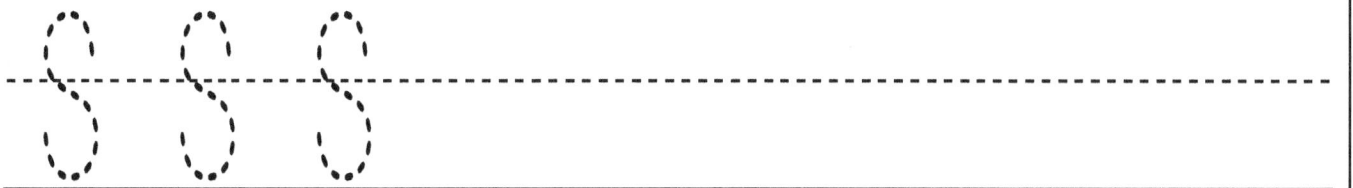

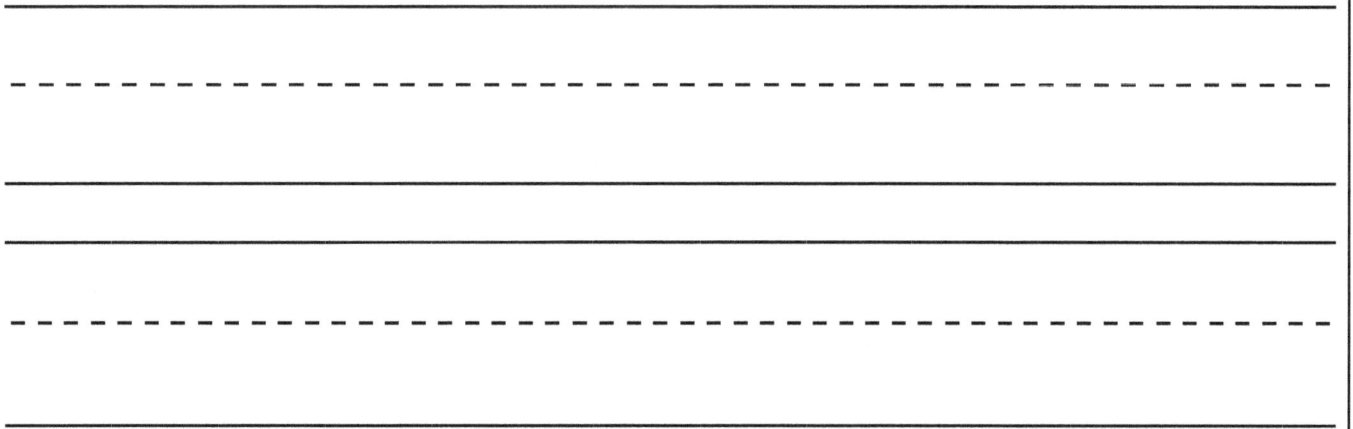

S S S S S S S S S S S S

S S S S

S S S

S

S

Name:_____ Date:_____

Trace each letter. Practice writing each letter on your own.

S S S S S S S S S S S S S

S S S S

S S S

S S

S

Name:_____ Date:_____

Trace each letter. Practice writing each letter on your own.

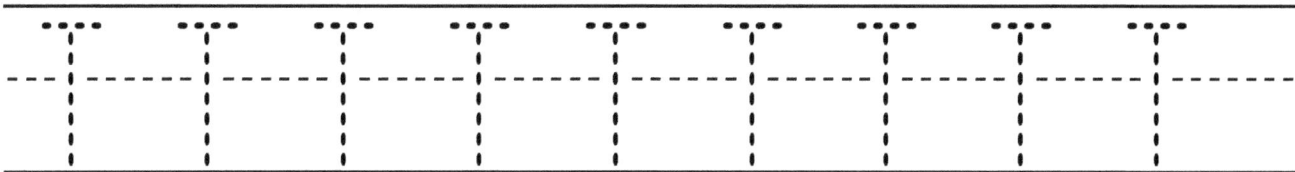

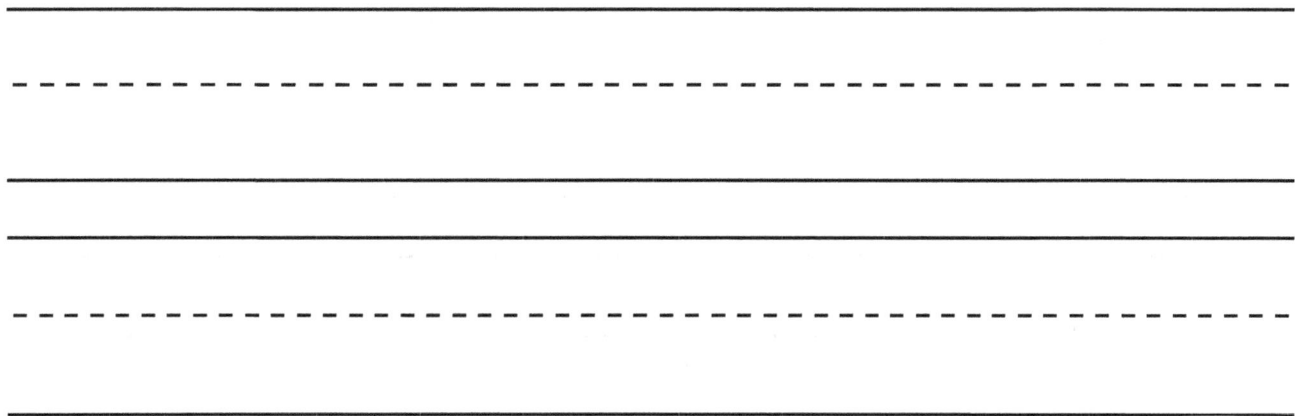

T T T T T T T T

T T T T

T T T

T T

T

Name:_____ Date:_____

Trace each letter. Practice writing each letter on your own.

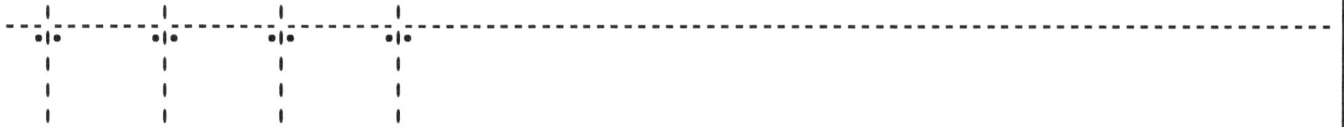

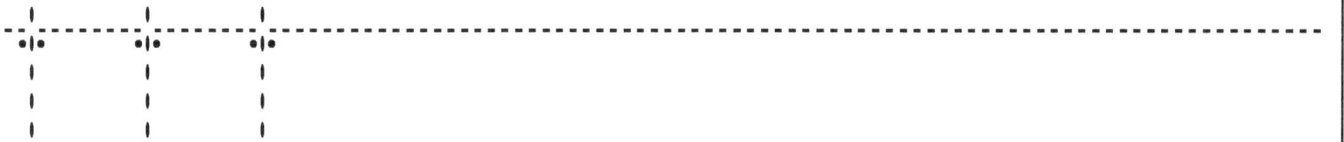

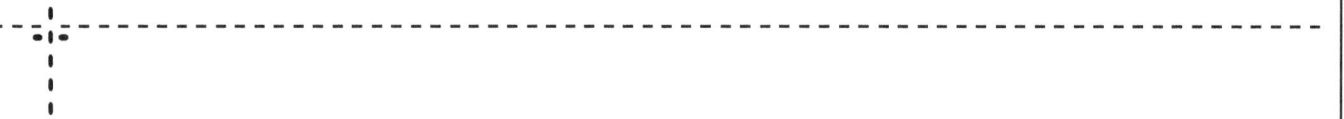

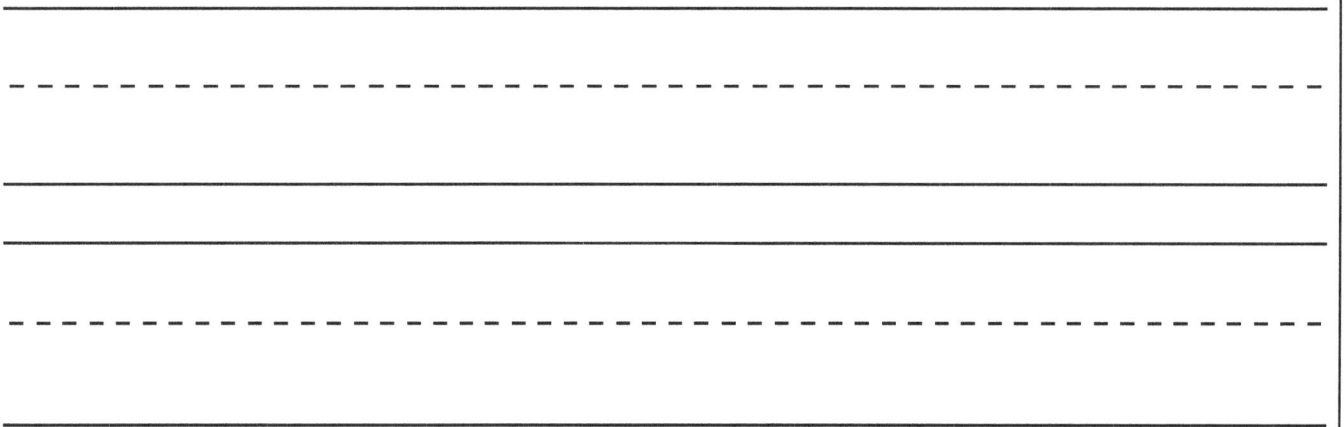

Trace each letter. Practice writing each letter on your own.

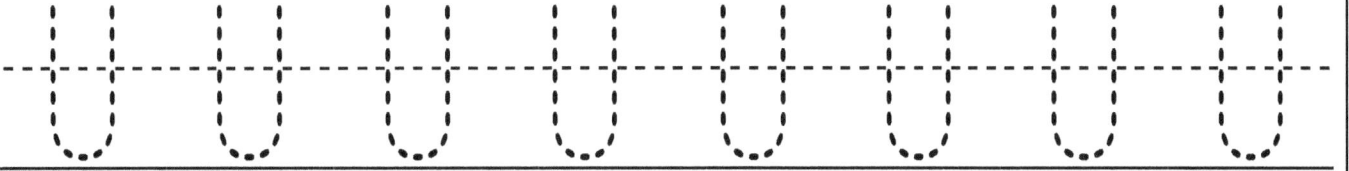

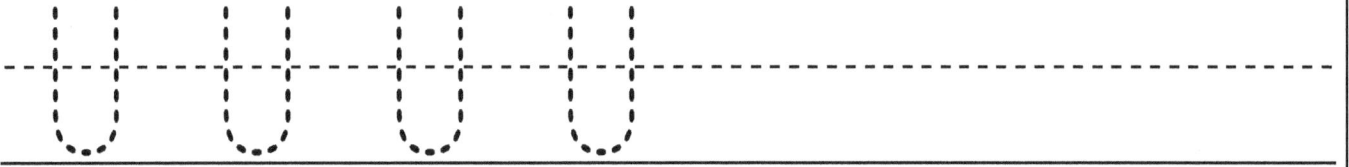

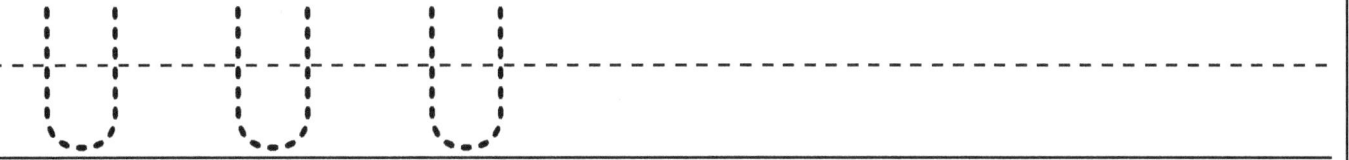

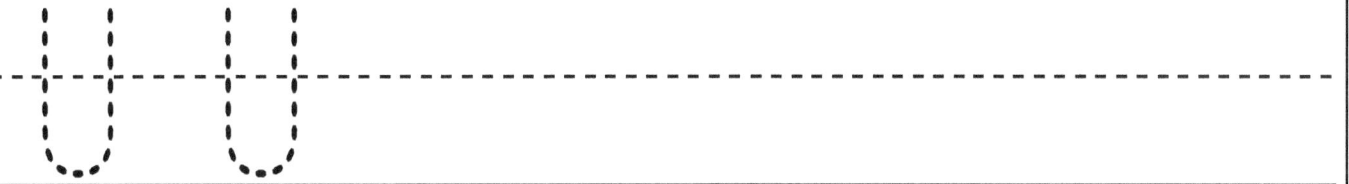

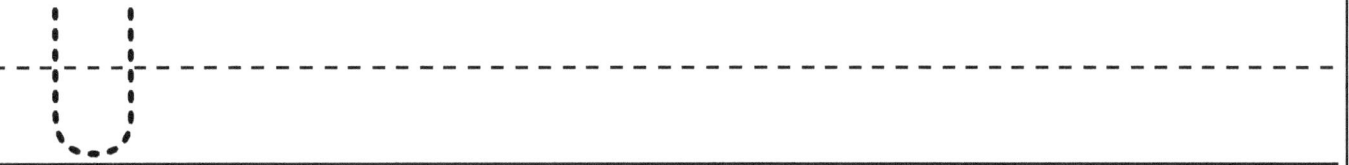

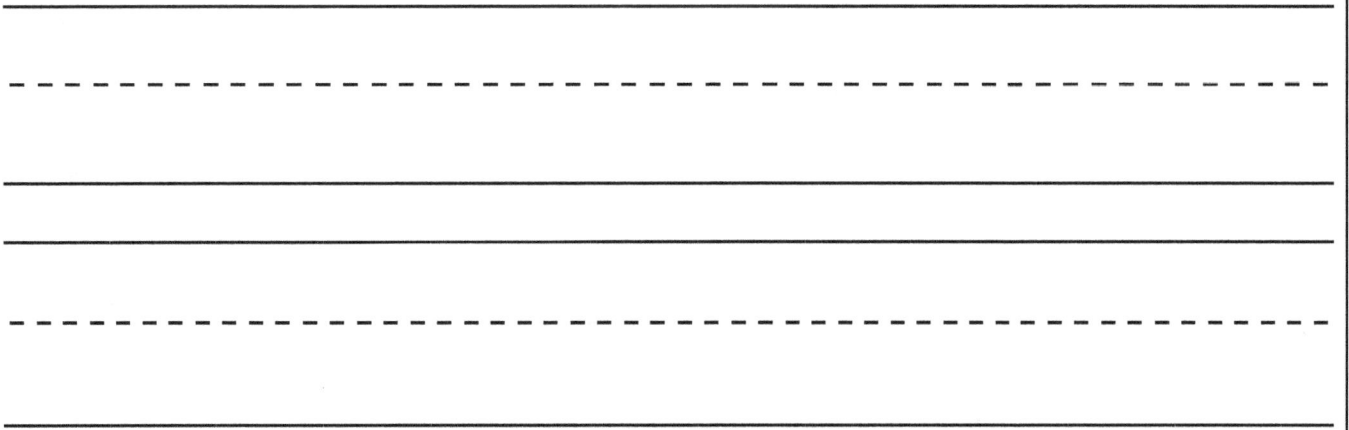

U U U U U U U U

U U U U

U U U

U U

U

Name:_____ Date:_____

Trace each letter. Practice writing each letter on your own.

U U U U U U U U U U U U U

U U U U

U U U

U U

U

Name:_____ Date:_____

Trace each letter. Practice writing each letter on your own.

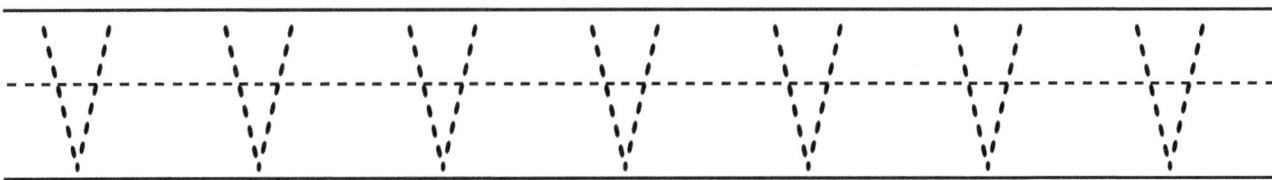

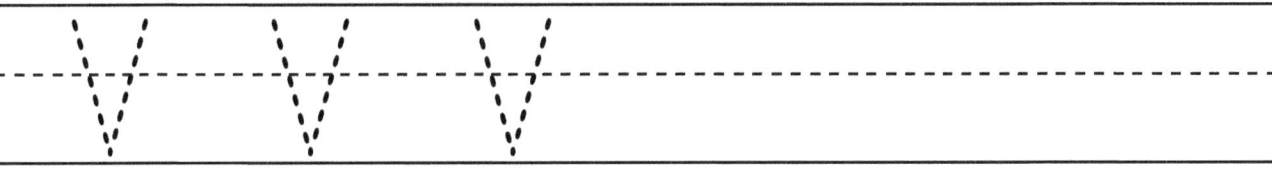

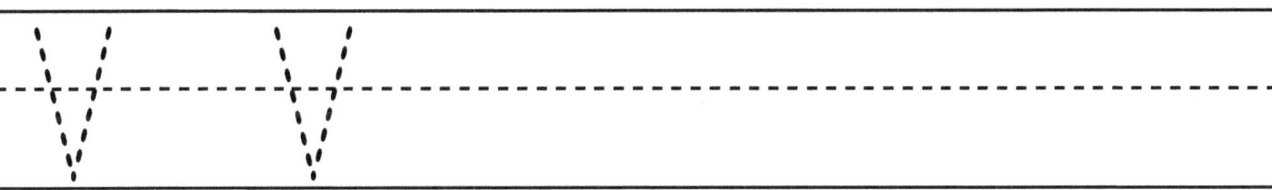

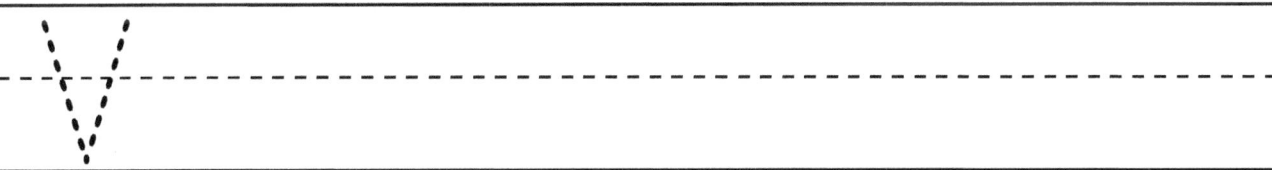

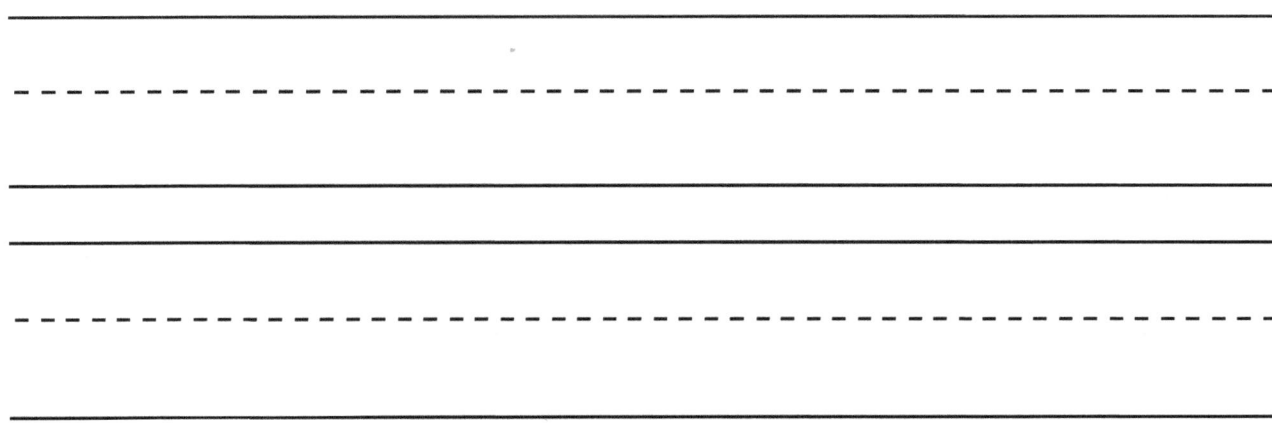

V V V V V V V

V V V V

V V V

V V

V

Trace each letter. Practice writing each letter on your own.

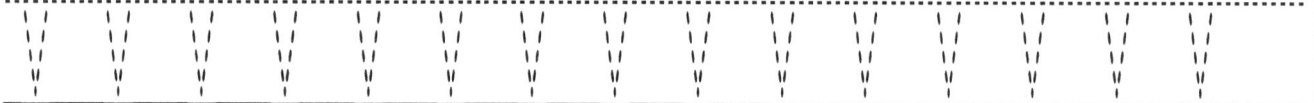

V V V V V V V V V V V V V V V V

V V V V

V V V

V V

V

Trace each letter. Practice writing each letter on your own.

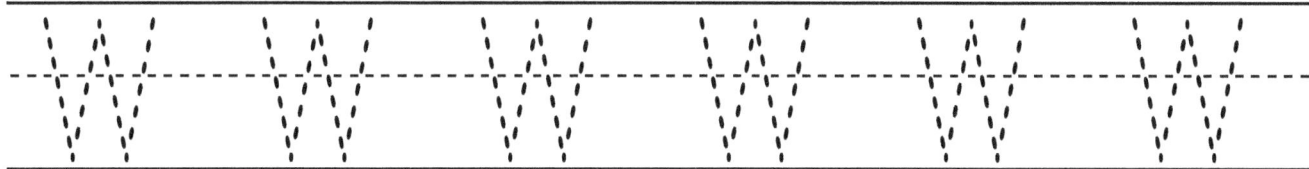

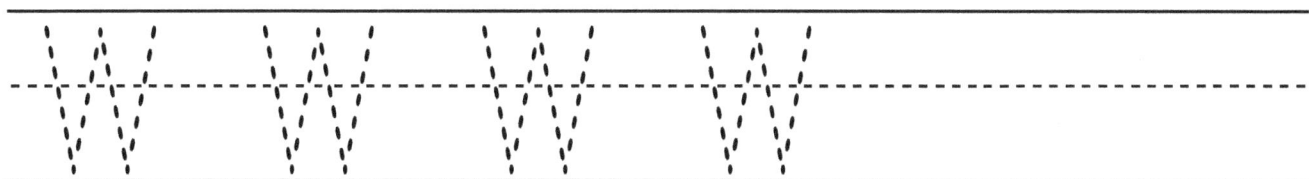

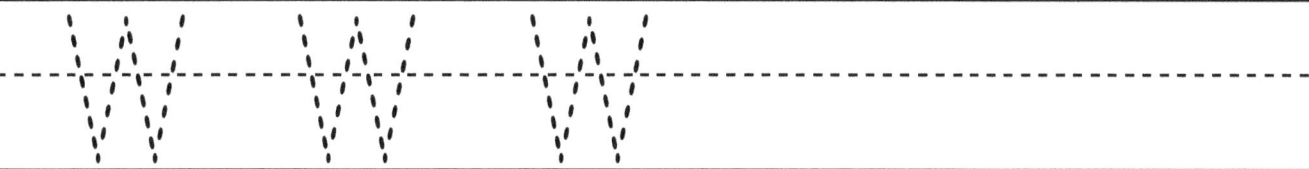

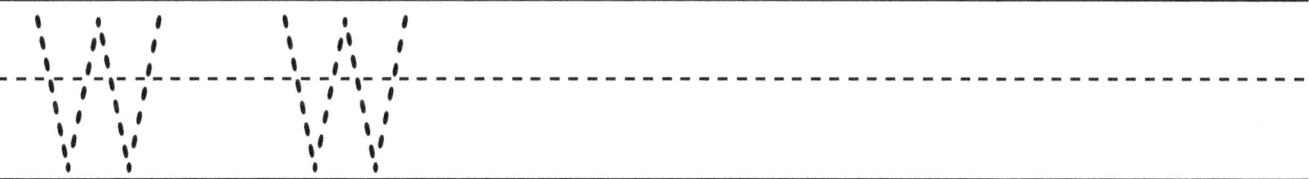

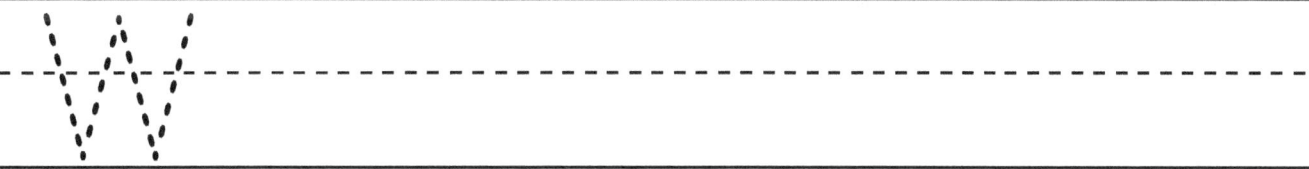

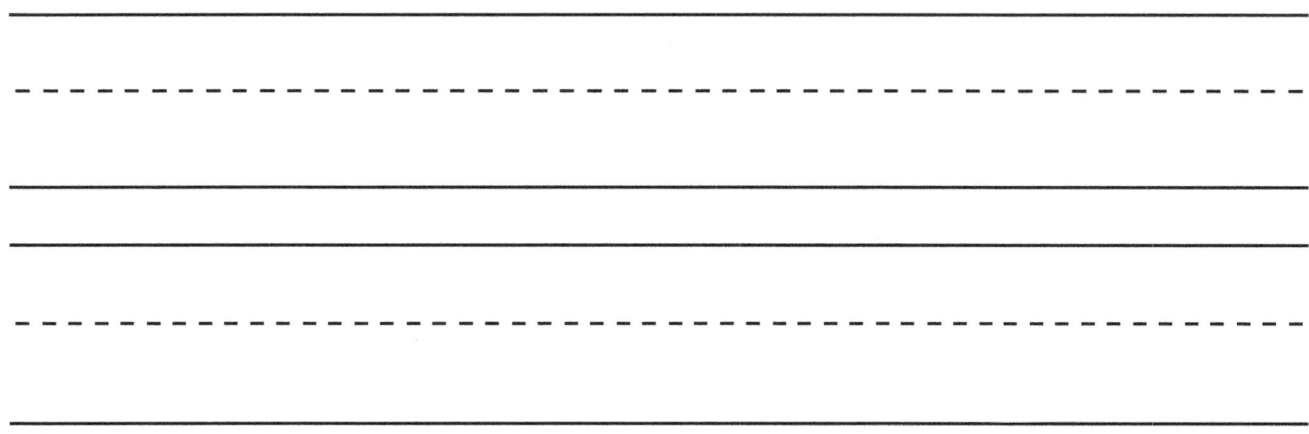

W W W W W W

W W W W

W W W

W W

W

Trace each letter. Practice writing each letter on your own.

W W W W W W W W W W W W

W W W W

W W W

W W

W

Name:_____ Date:_____

Trace each letter. Practice writing each letter on your own.

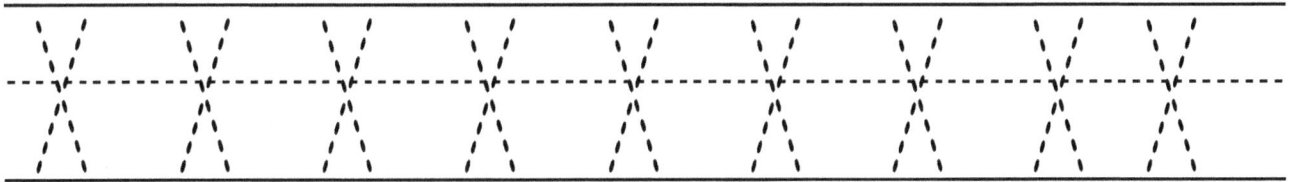

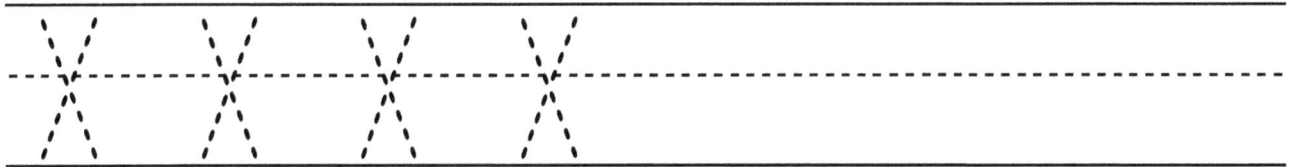

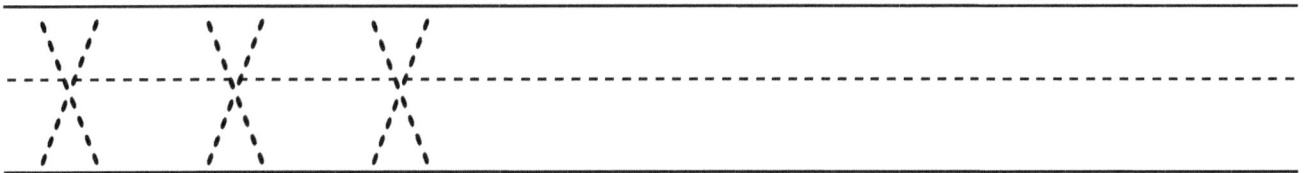

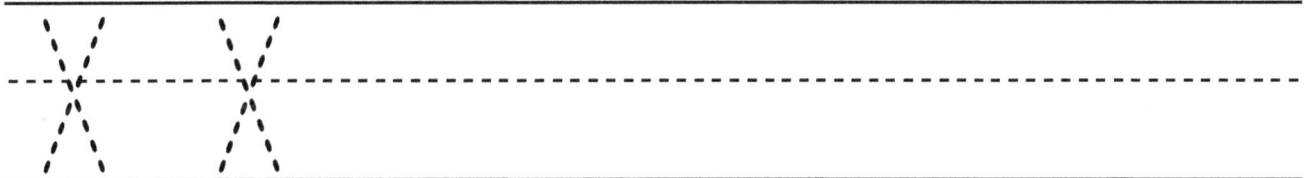

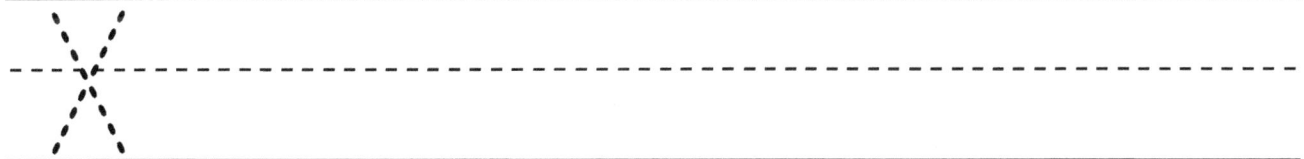

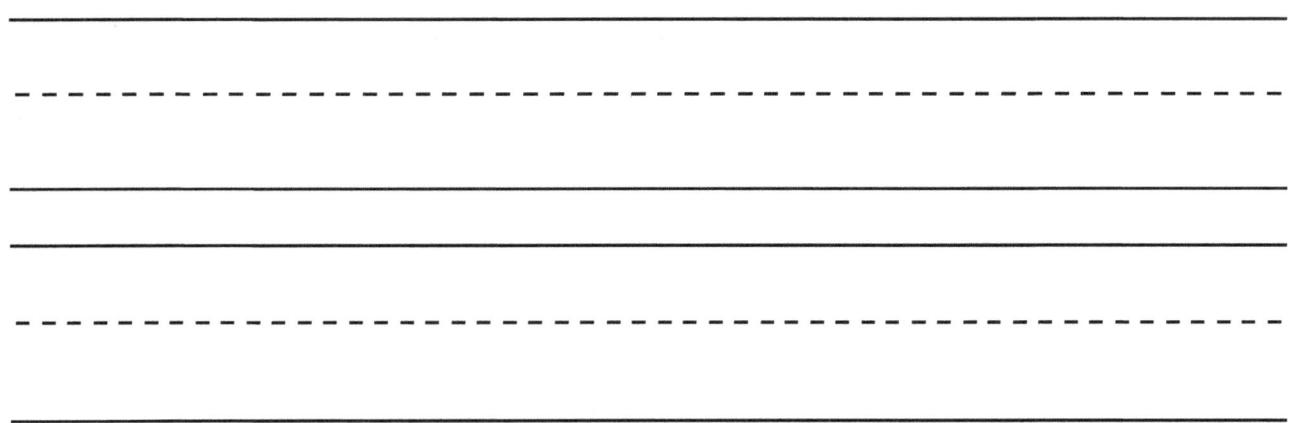

X X X X X X X X X

X X X X

X X X

X X

X

Trace each letter. Practice writing each letter on your own.

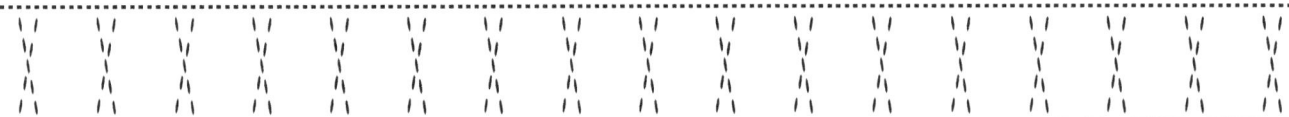

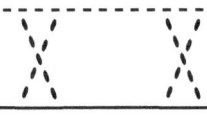

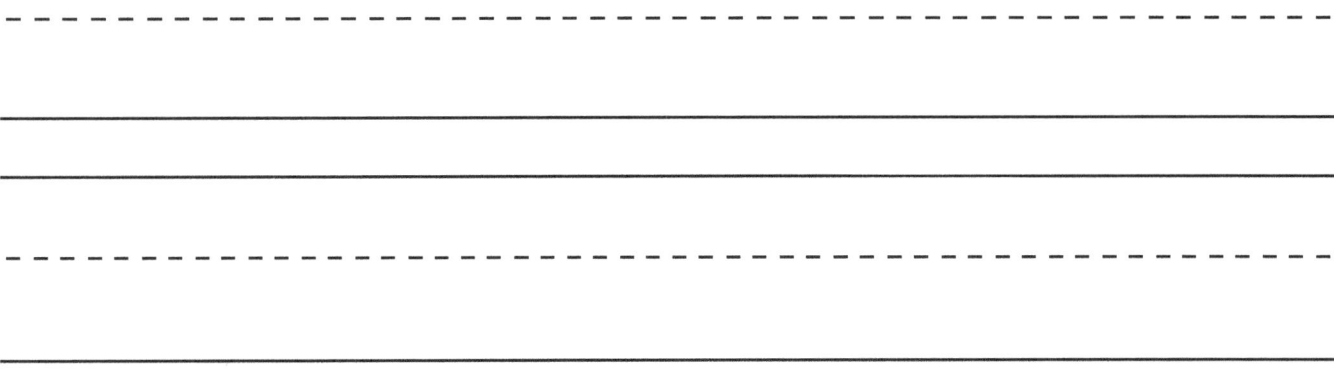

X X X X X X X X X X X X X X X X X X

X X X X

X X X

X X

X

Trace each letter. Practice writing each letter on your own.

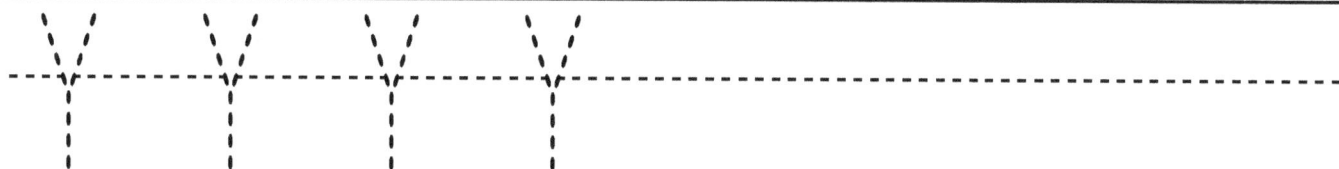

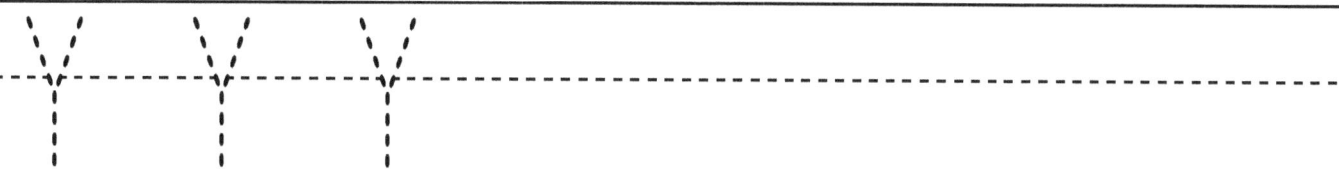

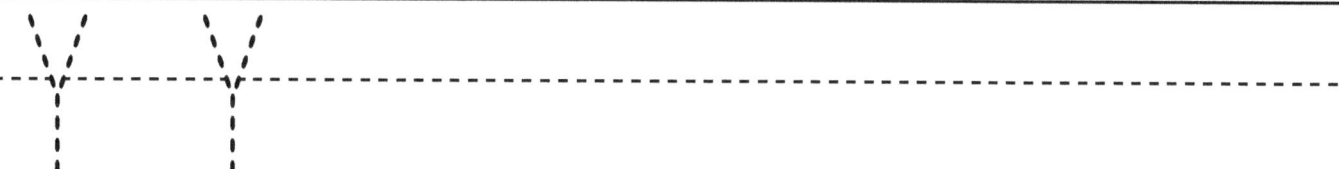

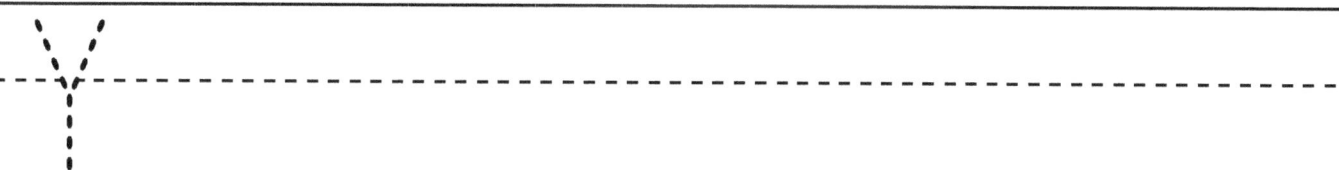

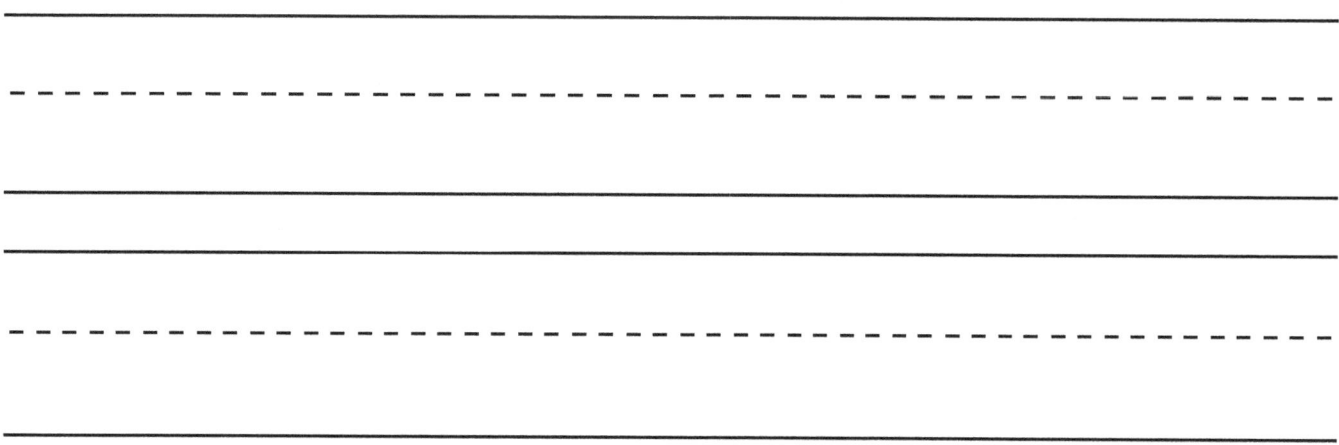

Y Y Y Y Y Y Y Y Y Y

Y Y Y Y

Y Y Y

Y Y

Y

Trace each letter. Practice writing each letter on your own.

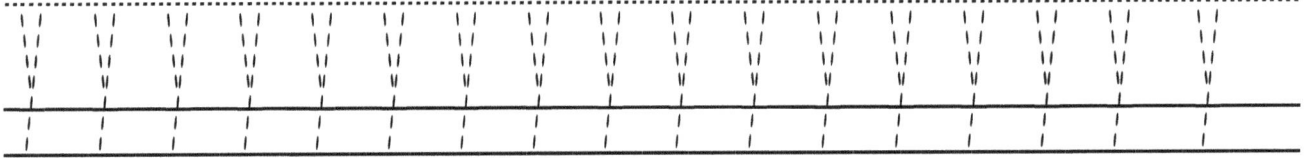

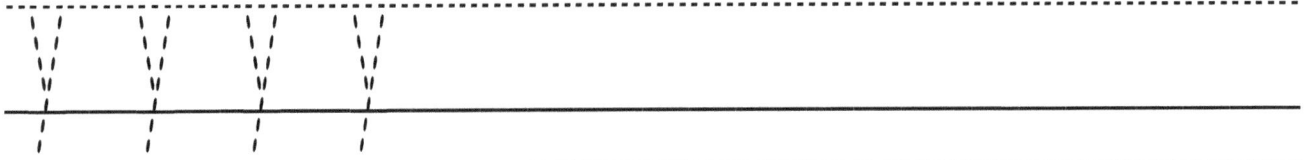

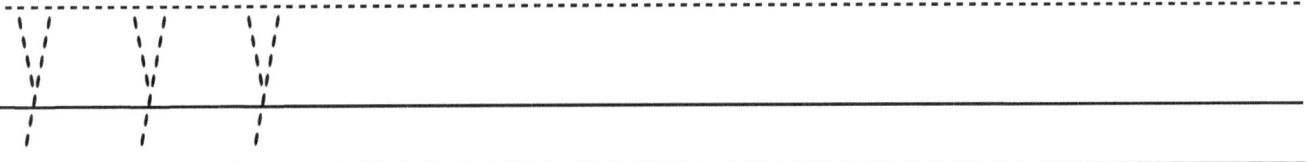

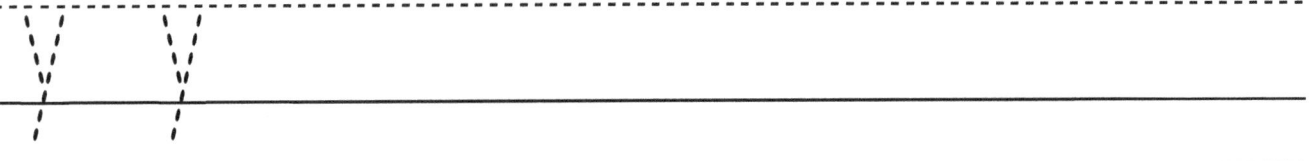

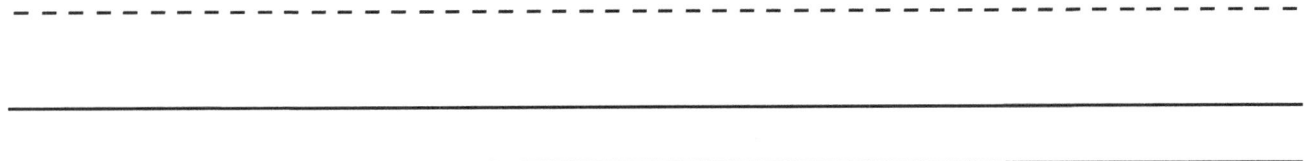

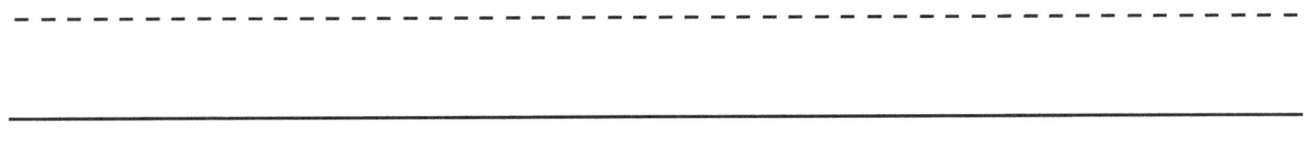

Name:_____ Date:_____

Trace each letter. Practice writing each letter on your own.

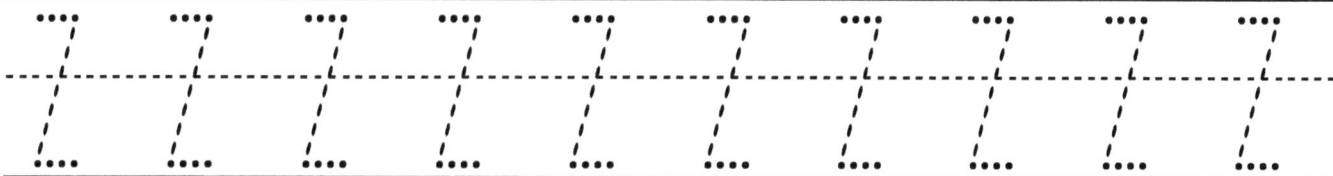

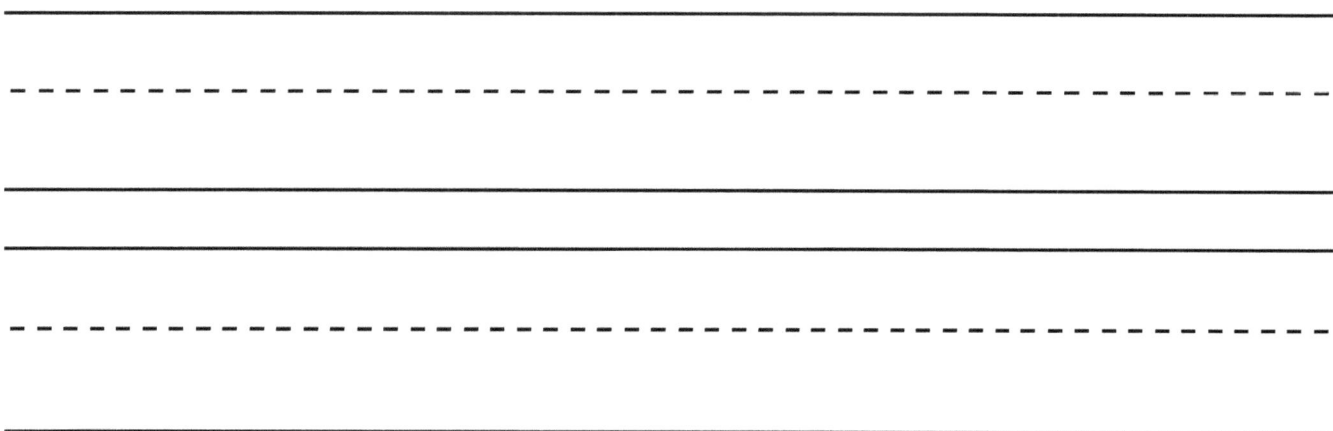

Z Z Z Z Z Z Z Z Z Z

Z Z Z Z

Z Z Z

Z Z

Z

Trace each letter. Practice writing each letter on your own.

Z Z Z Z Z Z Z Z Z Z Z Z Z Z Z Z Z

Z Z Z Z

Z Z Z

Z Z

Z

MOTIVATIONAL VOCABULARY

Courageous - Doing something even when you are scared or nervous.

Jewel - One that is highly steemed or precious.

Noble - Having or showing good character traits that other people admire.

Original - Being like yourself and not like others; unique.

Quintessential - A person who is a perfect example of something.

Unique - Being one of a kind; no other person is like you.

Victorious - Having won a victory and feeling a sense of fuifillment.

Witty - Someone or something that is funny and clever.

X-factor - A quality or unknown factor that makes someone or something more interesting or valuable.

Zestful - A person that has as an energertic and enthusiastic spirit.

MOTIVATIONAL VOCABULARY

DAILY POSITIVE AFFIRMATIONS

I AM AMAZING!
I AM BOLD!
I AM COURAGEOUS!
I AM DETERMINED!
I AM EXCELLENT!
I AM FANTASTIC!
I AM GIFTED!
I AM HONEST!
I AM INTELLIGENT!
I AM A JEWEL!
I AM KIND!
I AM LOVABLE!
I AM MAGNIFICENT!
I AM NOBLE!
I AM ORIGINAL!
I AM POWERFUL!
I AM QUINTESSENTIAL!
I AM RESPECTFUL!
I AM SPECIAL!
I AM TALENTED!
I AM UNIQUE!
I AM VICTORIOUS
I AM WITTY !
I AM A X-FACTOR!
I AM YOUTHFUL !
I AM ZESTFUL !